OXFORDSHIRE

Edited by Michelle Warrington

First published in Great Britain in 1999 by
YOUNG WRITERS
Remus House,
Coltsfoot Drive,
Woodston,
Peterborough, PE2 9JX
Telephone (01733) 890066

Copyright Contributors 1999

HB ISBN 0 75431 544 4
SB ISBN 0 75431 545 2

FOREWORD

Young Writers have produced poetry books in conjunction with schools for over eight years; providing a platform for talented young people to shine. This year, the Celebration 2000 collection of regional anthologies were developed with the millennium in mind.

With the nation taking stock of how far we have come, and reflecting on what we want to achieve in the future, our anthologies give a vivid insight into the thoughts and experiences of the younger generation.

We were once again impressed with the quality and attention to detail of every entry received and hope you will enjoy the poems we have decided to feature in *Celebration 2000 Oxfordshire* for many years to come.

CONTENTS

Our Lady's Convent Junior School

Laura Adams	54
Sophie Haverton	54
Richard King	55
Katy Cave	55
Olga Luscombe	56
Felicity Coles	56
Philippa Smith	57
Ben Green	57
Laura Dziewulski	58
Matthew Gottwald	58
Hannah Sarsfield-Hall	59
Nicola Mansell	59
Imogen Maund	60
William Peskett	60
Hayley Bater	61
Emily Owen	61
Gemma Allen	62
Victoria Barclay	62
Jessica Harris	63
Niamh Cahill	64

South Moreton Primary School

Kimberley Agostino	64
Jeremy Stockdale	65
Carmela Liverton	65
Ben Hordienko	66
Katherine Murphy	66
Alex Cracknell	67
Ben Gummery	67
Zoe Shuttleworth	68
Kerry-Anne Vaughan	69
Alice Maddox	69
Jocelyn Earl	69
Ruth Wollen	70
Nathan Butler	70
James Lineker	71
Nathan Randall	71

Ashley Stables	90
Charlotte Hooper	90
David Tompkins	90
Hannah Jones	91
Thomas Winwood	92
Robbie Davis	92
Charlotte Davies	93
Philip Platt	94
Adam Jones	94
Hannah Taylor	95
Kirsty Parrott	95
Jane Boreham	96
Emma Ealey	96
James Wartke-Dunbar	97
Phum Probets	97

Uffington Primary School

Thomas Lloyd	98
Karen Cooper	99
Martyn Fowler	99
Tom Cracknell	100
Jack Tilling	100
Jonathan Ambidge	101
Georgia Black	102
Tom Cooper	103
Georgie Baily	104
Jackie Watson	105
Dale Whitehorn	106
Robert Bowsher	106
Sarah Cooper	107
Sophie Bowsher	108
Charlotte Bond	109
Anita Preston	110
Michelle Gaffka	111

Wantage CE Junior School

Louise Goyder	112
Claire Humberstone	112

The Poems

BUTTERFLY

I'm a little butterfly
Proud of my wings
They are very colourful
I fly all day
I have a three course dinner
Insects
Flies
Insects
Afterwards I fly it off
Now I'm fine
I go to sleep and close my wings
I wonder what tomorrow will bring?

Matt Foster (9)
Aston Rowant Primary School

SPACE MAN

I'm going into
Outer space,
To try and help
The human race.
I'm trying to
Find out about
The moon.
It's goodbye
For now.
I'll see you soon.

Sophie Bright (9)
Aston Rowant Primary School

THE MAGIC SHOE BOX

I will put in the shoe box

The sound of a rainforest storm
Smoke from an Indian's camp fire
A horn of a unicorn.
I will put in the shoe box

The pluck of a sea horse's mane
A magnificent rainbow
The beak of a dodo.

I will put in the shoe box

A rumble of the Atlantic sea
An octopus's tentacle
And an eyelash from a rat

I shall dance in my shoe box
Till the night has played the tune away.

Emma Robinson (8)
Aston Rowant Primary School

CATS

Cats spend their lives dozing
Stretched out in front of the log fire,
Or legs folded away and tail tucked under,
Or curled up like a doughnut
On the window ledge.

Philippa Waldron (9)
Aston Rowant Primary School

A FISHY POEM

I am a fish
Living in the sea,
I love my life because
I am free
I've scales on my back
And a lovely shiny tail
I am definitely prettier
Than a humpback whale.
With my big round eyes
And shimmering skin
I am definitely cleaner
Than a newly bought pin.

Jenny Matthews (10)
Aston Rowant Primary School

SWIMMING POOL

I have loads of people in me today
But nobody to play with.
People have fun,
But no one talks to me.
They jump in the deep end,
And splash around the shallow.
Some swim lengths,
And some just wallow.

Anastasia Handl (8)
Aston Rowant Primary School

MY HAMSTER

She has a twitchy nose, and very sharp teeth.
Her eyes are as black as night and
Ears are small and white.
She's quite a tubby thing.
She loves to eat her food.
She has tiny feet and hands
And a stumpy little tail.
Her fur is soft as silk.
She's like a gymnast when she jumps off
Her house and runs about on her wheel.
Her name is Toffee and I love her very much.

Annabelle Bretton (9)
Aston Rowant Primary School

MY DOG SUZIE

My dog Suzie is a wonderful bitch
She does nothing but scratch
She does nothing but itch.
She sleeps all day she plays all night.
Her eyes are like big black golf balls
She is fast soft and cuddly, white and furry
And that's why she is my dog Suzie!

Joanne Dyer (9)
Aston Rowant Primary School

FISH

I squiggle I squirm and
All sorts of things
I sway and I swim
And I live underwater.
I blow bubbles of all kinds, big and small
I have fins that are delicate and
I use gills to breathe deep
Under the water.
I have lovely food and get fed once a day
I am all sorts of colours of blue
Gold and red
I swim under stones I get cleaned
Every fortnight
I'm as light as a feather for I am a fish.

Kristi Holiday (10)
Barley Hill Primary School

THE SNAKE

In the grass,
Slipping and sliding,
There was a snake,
No one was about,
The creature rose up,
The black hood flaring, fire in his eyes,
Jumping at the grass,
It slivered away eyes calming.

Hannah Johnston (9)
Barley Hill Primary School

WHALES!

Swimming slowly through the sea,
Oh, I do wish that were me,
Blowing spray, swirling fast,
Whales swim and glide,
> Whales are honest and
> Have nothing to hide,
> A mammal is what
> They are,
> Having the young that they
> Don't let far,
> Caring and warm blooded,
> Swimming through the sea like a mole,
> Then they go to the surface and blow through their hole,
> How the whale came to be,
> Really, really shocks me!

Helen Scholey (10)
Barley Hill Primary School

WEATHER

The rain raced down to the
Ground like a bird.
It ran across the pipe like
Someone in a race.

It made lakes and rivers.
The rain soaked up the grass,
People put on big big raincoats.

The next day the sun came out
Everybody put their hats on
It's sunny and hot, a right jolly old day.

Kayleigh Trafford (10)
Barley Hill Primary School

NIGHT FLY

When night sweeps over the world, the sky is completely pearled.
With sparkling white crystals, covering a blanket of dark blue velvet.
Stillness wraps everything in its glare, while glistening jewel bright
eyes dwell there.
Darkness falls from the heavens, while pitching everything in shining
fireflies
Everything is blacked out of sight, by stars and silence from the night.
Fear clutches the human mind with pain, while ghoulish white light
washes over land.
In the distance birds fly away, waiting for the sunrise to bring the day.
Fish swim through clear blue water, with a shining white sphere
reflected.
Deep in the night's deathly air, roams an insane brown bear.
It puts its head to the moonlit sky, and roars away with an echo like
thunder
Then overhead it looks and spies and sees at last the morning sunrise!
The moon goes down and yellow beams, peep over the edge of the
crystal clear water.
The sun rises higher and higher over the world, and the night is up
curled.
Goodbye night fly! Goodbye!

Madeleine Fry (9)
Barley Hill Primary School

THE SILVER WEB

Sparkling in the corner of the tree is a
                              spider's web
And on the sparkling web is a spider,
It is as black as a cloud ready to burst.
All curled up.

I point a sharp finger at it thinking and
Sinking into the snow at the same time
Am I going to touch it.

I think.
I hate spiders
Moving closer . . . getting more scared
I push it off the web
It's still moving it quickly scurries off.

I tread back
I look up. Ahhh!
I run off.

A few weeks later I go back out
There's a spider in a tree spinning a
                              silver web.

Sarah Wilmer (10)
Barley Hill Primary School

SNAKE

The snake, he slithers
Scraping his scaly body across the scorching sand,
Sending spits and snaps at you
Flicking his slimy tongue through his sharp and shiny
                              teeth.

He slithers silently searching for lunch,
Snapping, snipping and snarling he snaps free his
                    jaws from a slain deer,
He swallows it selfishly not leaving any
                    remains of his stolen meal.

Ben McKeown (9)
Barley Hill Primary School

THE WEATHER

The rain is stormy
When will it last.
The rain is heavy
Don't stay go away.

Let it be sunny
Let it be hot
Please, please,
Not rain.

The wind is bad,
It will blow your
Coats off.
The wind is powerful
It will blow your
Fence down.

The rain had past
It won't come again
I'll make sure of that.

Jade Kotvics (9)
Barley Hill Primary School

WIND

The wind was blowing furiously.
Wind over here and wind everywhere,
The trees trickled side to side
Then crack! It snapped.
Then another and another.
Then the aerial on the tele flickered
Then snap it went off
The car was moving an inch,
Then bang smash it had gone.
The door rattled then creak,
It had opened.
A scream! A bang,
The radio blew up,
Then it was silent.

Mark Dowthwaite (10)
Barley Hill Primary School

NEW

Will there be a car that
Will go at the speed of light?
Will there be children who will
Stay up late at night?
Will there be penguins deciding to stay here?
Will there be a new Nintendo Gear?
Will I wish for a new fish
What will we do?
Will everything be new.

James Rhodes (8)
Ferndale Prep School

THE UNIVERSE

Time is drifting through the universe,
It's the millennium soon,
New things will be happening,
It sounds good the millennium.

Time is drifting quickly,
Nearly the millennium,
I just can't wait,
Till the millennium.

What will life be like,
I do not know,
Will it be fun,
Or boring.

Time is drifting through the universe,
It's the millennium soon,
New things will be happening,
It sounds good the millennium.

Charlotte Brooks (8)
Ferndale Prep School

MILLENNIUM

Yes! The millennium,
We'll have genetically modified food probably!
Millennium Eve when parties will be out,
Hopefully we'll be on the moon.

If we did,
Would the aliens like us?
Would they not?
Got to go and see.

Samuel Welch (8)
Ferndale Prep School

THE YEAR 2000

In the year 2000
For all that I know
We might be
Allied with some
Most extra special people

In the year 2000
We might have robots
That could run and play
And could help us
In all we do

I sometimes think
What Henry VIII would
Have done in the year 2000
Would he chop people's heads off
Or would he be nice?
I wonder what he would do

In the year 2000
Will we change our currency
Will it be Euro or some other
Like Francs or American bucks
I have no idea at all.

Ben Prior (9)
Ferndale Prep School

COMING

Coming to 2000
I hope we have
Flying bikes
What will the sea be like?
Flying surf-boards!

Will we eat starfish?
What will houses be like?
Will we see the sun?
Will there be clouds?

Marc Johnson (8)
Ferndale Prep School

PAST AND PRESENT

We are cutting forests,
We are eating trees,
We are drinking petrol,
Not a cup of tea,
Just guessing!

Now there are no lorries,
Now there are no cars,
But I am on a shuttle,
Speeding through the stars,
Hurry!

Animals have clothing,
Animals have cars,
Animals have power,
And a language just like ours
Oh yes!

Do people like the present
Or did they like the past,
Time is going onwards,
Really, really fast.
We'll never have the past again,
We'll never have the past,
So let us love each moment,
For soon our time will pass.

Jonathan Moss (8)
Ferndale Prep School

THE YEAR 2000

The year 2000 may be a
New creation.
Next year is year 2000
Let's have a celebration.

Next year will be a
Wonderful year,
Come on everybody
With me cheer.

What will year 2000
Be like?
I don't know
Do you?

Emily Redman (9)
Ferndale Prep School

THE YEAR 2000

In the year 2000,
Will it all be the same,
Or will the animals talk to us
Like woof, miaow or neigh.

In the year 2000,
Will our food taste the same,
Or will it taste of slugs and flies,
The answer I cannot say.

The year 2000 seems so exciting,
From what I've heard that is,
If dogs talk and horses too,
Then I cannot wait to see it.

Marie-Louise McCrea (8)
Ferndale Prep School

WHAT WILL HAPPEN

In the year two thousand
Changes might be in the air
Some drinks might not be sold
Ribena, orange, tea and milk
Or they'll be really old

In the year two thousand
Will chocolate be chocolate?
Will it be brown?
Will it be dark or light?
And will it still taste the same

In the year two thousand
Will there be names?
If there are will they be funny?
Will they be normal or will they be strange?
I wish I knew what will happen

Sarah Morton (8)
Ferndale Prep School

TWO THOUSAND YEARS SINCE HE WAS HERE

The days have gone by
And so have the years.
Two thousand years since the Peacemaker was here;
But peace has gone away
Leaving us to battle, war and jealousy
Two thousand years that was
But I believe the Peacemaker will come again.

Daniel Rhodes (8)
Ferndale Prep School

21ST CENTURY

The millennium's coming,
Like a balloon in the breeze
It's bobbing, it's bumping
And freely galumping
We don't know what it's like

The 1900's are going
Like a ship sailing in a storm
It's tossing it's turning
It's mast-heads they are burning
Will they invent a four-wheeled bike?

Just think when the millennium's going
What will've happened by then?
They may have invented plastic men
We don't know what it's like.

Jeremy Owen (8)
Ferndale Prep School

THE TIME AT NIGHT

Time is running through the world,
In the light of day,
It turns the world around
And then it goes away.
At night it's very spooky,
Ghosts come out and play,
And when I go to bed at night
I always jump away,
From the man who lives under the bed,
Who nibbles your toes away!

Emily Marchant (9)
Ferndale Prep School

THE MILLENNIUM

The millennium is coming soon,
Soon we will be living on the moon.
It's time to celebrate,
Jesus' 2000th birthday.
And, I suppose we will have to shout Hooray.
Will we eat plastic?
What will it be like in the Millennium Dome?
Will the world be covered in foam?
I wonder, what will the world be like?
Especially if we invent a flying bike.
Will the world be invaded by Wonka Doddles?
(What are they?)
Are they people made out of hay?
Will we go flying out of the galaxy,
In a doodle
(What is that?)
Alright,
It's a supersonic hen.
Will we invent a time machine?
Or, will I wake up and find it's all a dream?
So we will have to wait and see,
Who will be the first man to have a baby?
Will we start life again?
This time on Mars.
Will I be able to eat the Mars Bars?
Will we start life again?
Or will I just say,
Let's celebrate.

Alex Jordan (9)
Ferndale Prep School

YEAR 3000

Very strange,
Very strange creature,
Half rhino half lion,
With chameleon colours,
Very strange.

Very strange,
No humans here,
Driven out by robots,
That come from this polluted world,
Very sad.

Very strange,
All the trees gone,
No countryside left,
More types of pollution than ever,
Nasty.

Go home,
Go right back home,
And stay there forever,
I clamber into my time machine,
Go home.

Lucy McGregor (9)
Freeland CE Primary School

YEAR 3000

Cars are going by
Their wheels are high
The lorries go past me
Buildings all around me
Spaceships everywhere
Cars floating across me
Thousands and thousands in the air
floating by.

Michael Thompson (8)
Freeland CE Primary School

CLOTHES IN THE YEAR 2000

Funny shapes
Lots of colours
Lots of funny hats and coats
Lots of big hats with feathers on weird shapes.

Sarah Moore (8)
Freeland CE Primary School

JOBS IN THE YEAR 2000

Engineers are busy in the year 2000 fixing and mending all kinds
Of machines, twisting and turning their tods.
Men at work are making machinery and bits and bobs.
People at petrol stations make petrol for customers.
Builders are busy in the year 2000 building and filling gaps
in houses.

Lewis Dix (8)
Freeland CE Primary School

New Future

Ships are at the docks.
Trains come 30 miles an hour.
Submarines change orange red.
Buses have bubbles inside.
Bikes have gigantic wheels.
Cars have electric motors.
Motor bikes go slowly along the
                                    slippery roads.
Lorries jerk across the motorway
Trucks go to adventurous places.
Boats go faster in the countryside.

Lee Vanstone (8)
Freeland CE Primary School

Sport In 2000

Rugby

Prism-shaped balls fly through the air
With brand new boots made by Nike Air

Rally

Flashing coloured cars race at 100,000 mph
Down the race track with
A lot of great extreme power.

Tom Lewis (8)
Freeland CE Primary School

YEAR 3000

Robots
Lights on their heads
Wires in their bodies
Robots are police officers
Robots

Fast trains
Fast floating trains
No tracks to travel on
People in trains are very ill
Fast trains

New chairs
Chairs are floating
Chairs with auto warmer
Chairs can float in the stadium
Cool chairs.

Cars zoom
Cars float then zoom
Cars never ever crash
Cars don't need petrol any more
Cars fly.

Paul Jacobs (9)
Freeland CE Primary School

WATERFALL

The water of the waterfall
Splashes rocks top to bottom
Fish jump wave to wave
Fish get washed up onto the shore
Leaves fall into the water
Fall and flow away
Then the waves slow down
And the water dries up
The waterfall turns into
A play den for children.

Rachel Smith (8)
Freeland CE Primary School

MILLENNIUM YEAR 2000

Millennium,
Year 2000.
I can't wait till year 2000.
Digital clocks
More to learn,
More programmes,
To watch on TV
More money invented
But it's only millennium year
2000
Fantastic toys
Better shows,
The happier the world will
Get as it grows.
All because of millennium
year 2000.

Olivia Lucas-Ulyat (9)
Hornton County Primary School

A Millennium Party

The party that flows in a friendly atmosphere.
The ring of the bell,
The murmur of voices
That hits Mr Fell.
The fizz of the drinks
The pop of the cork,
The whiz of a motorbike
Out where you walk,
The crunch of the crisps,
The shout of a mum,
The bell on a bike,
The call of a chum,
The friendly old man,
The strike of a clock as it dings 12 o'clock,
At last it's here,
The millennium's here,
Now it's time, *yes*,
'Old Lang Syne'.

Jess Wain (10)
Hornton County Primary School

Bug Enters Computer

What computer thinks?
Bug settles in home.
Computer is mad.
Computer gets hot.
Fizz goes the fuse.

Charles Hesketh (9)
Hornton County Primary School

NIGHT BUG

The midnight strike has begun,
Computer to computer.
Sweeping through the diskdrives,
The silent present running free.

The deadly demolisher,
Round the world.
Computers crashing,
Drives smashing.

The millennium monster
Into the net.
E-mailed through the night,
It is the bug.

We gave it computers,
Now it won't let us have them back!

Paul Rowe-Jones (10)
Hornton County Primary School

MILLENNIUM BUG

Hi! I'm the Millennium Bug.
I'll mess up your PC
I'll fiddle with the wires
And scramble up the screen.
I only come every millennium
Because it's mostly got noughts.
Your PC will be real confused
But if too fizzed out it will not be used,
Until the year 2001!

Niall MacKellar (10)
Hornton County Primary School

PRELUDE TO A NEW MILLENNIUM

I open my eyes.
The cockerel crows,
The wind blows,
In the morning sun.

A creaking mouse,
In the house,
Makes the prelude fun.

The immortal rapture of
Another thousand years,
Now the voices,
The loud voices,
Take the lead of the song.

The beat of the drumming rain,
Taking the rhythm on the window pane,
The day grows on,
Every note of the song.

The death of the sun
The end of the day,
The end of the song,
The light away.

Tom Hannah (9)
Hornton County Primary School

I WANT TO BE A FAMOUS POET

I want to be a poet when I get older.
In my room I have a folder.
Compiled with poems I have written.
About famous people, even kittens!

I think that poets are quite rich.
My English teacher is a witch.
She wouldn't help me with my ambition,
So I've come to a decision.

I'm not going to be a poet when I grow up
Because I've got school work and I'm all muddled up
It's to write a poem about the millennium phenomenon
And it's a really big problem

I don't know anything about the millennium phenomenon
Onamatapia, alliteration how can I cope with them?
It's for a competition and I really want to win
But I can't seem to make the poem rhyme at all.

The other people at my school,
Have written poems and they're really cool
So I don't think I'll win, but no fear
Never mind, there's always next year.

Bethany Ponsford (10)
Hornton County Primary School

MR MILLENNIUM

My mum says there's someone coming
The tragic Millennium Bug.
He has the body of a caterpillar
He's the colour of a slug.

He lives in the computer
And eats potato-chips.
I think he's very friendly -
I'm sure he never nips.

He sleeps all day,
He comes out at night.
He's never ever grumpy,
He squeals with delight!

The news is going on and on
Of how evil this bug is,
But I know quite different,
He's a cool computer whiz!

He's also known as 'Mr Millennium'
Or Sir if I recall,
So he's been personally invited
To my millennium ball!

Jessica Wright (10)
Hornton County Primary School

MILLENNIUM BUG

My name's Millie the Millennium Bug,
So I'm going to crash the computer at countdown,
So at the date,
I'll be eating chips.
I'm Millie who crashes computers.

I'm going to bust the boy's box,
Because I'm as sly as a fox
Imagine what will happen to all the planes, heaters.
Everything I hope this isn't a bug free computer!

It's December 31st!
One more day to go,
I'm not in yet, but I will be.
Hang on, what does that sticker say?
And what are they saying?
Ahhhhh! Not a virus scanner! Pop! Ow!

Libby Edgar (8)
Hornton County Primary School

MILLENNIUM BUG?

Is it a caterpillar that crawls across the screen?
Is it a spider that plays with the wires?
Is it a cockroach that goes scratch scratch
Scratch in the computer?
Is it a snail that slithers on the wires?
Is it a ladybird that makes the screen go red?
Is it an insect that fiddles with the noughts?
Of course it's the Millennium Bug!

Samuel Offord (8)
Hornton County Primary School

THE MILLENNIUM

Big Ben strikes 12,
The millennium is here,
Feasting . . . . fasting,
Men drinking beer.
Where four thousand years ago, on this very spot,
A cave man sat,
By a fire, yellow and hot.
He'd have been hunting in the woods all day,
While we order our food on the Internet,
And sleep it away.

Modern technology goes straight to the brain,
Whiz computers and the underground trains,
Amazing medicines to cure aches and pains.
Global warming makes it hot and wet,
We call each other names like 'Twit' and 'Teacher's pet'.
Who knows what the future may hold -
A new source of power?
Or ice and cold?

Matthew Lucas-Ulyat (11)
Hornton County Primary School

HORRIFYING LIMERICKS

I was dancing in an old
School room when a vampire
Appeared on a broom.
So I screamed out boo
And squirted out glue
And he went back
Into his tomb.

Oliver Davidson (9)
Horspath Primary School

PLAYGROUND POEM

'Line up everyone' said Miss Glasson
'Remember don't drop litter!
I've got to clean the rabbits out.'
Let's play draughts
Pick teams pick teams
Let's get the basketballs out
I've got to get my snack
It's our turn on the play equipment.
        Time to go in.

Sophie Smith (8)
Horspath Primary School

PLAYGROUND POEM

People playing basketball, people swapping food
People playing running cakes on the move
People playing Game Boys, people in a mood
People playing and people being rude.

Robert Harper (8)
Horspath Primary School

HORRIFYING LIMERICK

I was on duty in the look out room.
When a zombie walked out of the gloom.
I covered him in glue.
And hid in the loo.
Now he's back in his horrifying tomb.

James Bedford (9)
Horspath Primary School

PLAYGROUND POETRY

Going out at playtime is the best part of our day,
But it's best in May,
Chewing chocolate,
Telling jokes,
Throwing balls,
People's calls,
Sticky lollies,
Children's dollies,
That's the best part of our day.

Ruth Lamont (9)
Horspath Primary School

MUMMY

M y mum is very loving.
U nderstanding mum
M agic mum
M erry mum
Y ou are the best.

Caitlin Bedford (7)
Horspath Primary School

MY MUM

M um you're great!
Y ou make me smile

M agnificent,
U seful.
M arvellous mum!

Madeleine Amos (7)
Horspath Primary School

MUMMY

My mum is lovely and she is wonderful too.
You are a young mum

Marvellous mum
Useful mummy
Mad mummy
Magic mummy
You are so thoughtful.

Emma Peachey (6)
Horspath Primary School

MY MUMMY

M y mum is marvellous
Y ou are beautiful

M y mum is funny
U seful for homework
M um is nice to me
M um I love you
Y ou are lovely.

Arron Eeley (7)
Horspath Primary School

MY MUM

M agical.
O ne kind person in my family.
T he best person in the world
H er eyes are wonderful
E xcellent
R eally loving.

Peter Allen (7)
Horspath Primary School

MY MUM

M arvellous mum.
Y oung mum.

M arvellous to me.
U nderstanding mum.
M arvellous to your family.

Francesca Parsons (8)
Horspath Primary School

MY MUM

M y mum is lovely
Y et she is angry when I am naughty

M agnificent!
U seful!
M arvellous mum
M um is excellent
Y es she is wonderful.

John Young (7)
Horspath Primary School

MARVELLOUS MOTHER

M arvellous.
O nly the best mothers are called Sue.
T ingling with kindness,
H ome is warm with you in it,
E xtremely kind and loving,
R oses are like you.

Kate Richards (7)
Horspath Primary School

MOTHER

M y mum is good to me because she got me a hamster.
O nly the best mum in the world.
T he animals love her.
H ave a lovely Mother's Day
E xtremely loving
R eally thoughtful.

Rebecca McKinlay (7)
Horspath Primary School

MY MOTHER

M y mum is wonderful.
O nly my mum is the best.
T he best mum in the world.
H appy person.
E xtremely kind.
R ather special to me.

Maddy Little (7)
Horspath Primary School

MOTHER

M y mother is intelligent.
O nly the best mum in the world.
T amara is beautiful.
H ave a lovely Mother's Day.
E aster is my mum's best time
R ight my mum for me.

Hailey Munt (7)
Horspath Primary School

MUMMY

M arvellous Mum.
U seful Mum.
M ake-up looks good.
M agnificent Mum.
Y ell out Mum's the boss.

Joanne Montgomery (6)
Horspath Primary School

MY MUM

M y mum is beautiful
Y ou are the best.

M agnificent mum
U tterly kind
M um is cool.

George Dugdale (8)
Horspath Primary School

MUMMY

M y mum is lovely
U nderstanding
M y mum is happy
M um is fun
Y ou are beautiful.

Ben Shepherd (6)
Horspath Primary School

JULIET - MY MUM

J uliet is like an armchair
U seful mummy is a friend
L ovely mummy is kind
I ntelligent mummy
E xtremely beautiful
T easing mummy

Sarah Nixey (7)
Horspath Primary School

MY MUMMY

M ummy I love you
U seful mummy
M agical mummy
M y mummy is wonderful
Y ou're the best mummy in the world.

Charles Robertson (6)
Horspath Primary School

MOTHER

M y mum is very beautiful.
O nly my mum is the best.
T he best mum I have ever had.
H as beautiful shiny hair.
E aster is the best time for her.
R ight mum for me.

Fiona Cranston (6)
Horspath Primary School

BENJAMIN POT

Once I was bullied
But now I'm not
When I was,
It was by
Benjamin Pot.
He followed me around
All day
And at night I
Had nightmares
About what he would
Do next
Benjamin Pot
I hate him a lot.

Tom Harper (11)
Horspath Primary School

THE CHASE

Chasing after me, at twenty miles per hour
The gang, with also, bully McGower
I glanced back and suddenly I felt myself go thud
They circled around and blocked my escape.
Then they covered my mouth with tape
And pulled my hair and said it was fake.

Then the teacher came out to ring the bell,
They said some last words and told me I smell
I thought about them all day and all night
And tried to get to sleep but it was a very hard fight.
The question kept going through my head
I couldn't find the answer
Was it that my hair was red?

Matthew Chase & Patrick Amos (11)
Horspath Primary School

THE BULLY

There I was stood in the street
Waiting for my friends to meet.
There with them were another gang,
Then suddenly there was a big bang.
Then came over another boy
There with him was his mate Troy.
Then I felt something on my back
I turned around and got a great wack.

My face really hurt so I ran and ran
There stood behind me a very kind man.
I ignored him and just ran and ran,
I got home and had nobody to turn to
But Stan. Stan was my pet dog.
I say to him every day
You're my mate don't ever go away.

Jenny Rees & Michaela Bond (11)
Horspath Primary School

MY MUM

M arvellous.
U nderstanding
M y mum's fantastic
M y mum's friendly.
Y ou are kind and helpful.

Ross Fletcher (7)
Horspath Primary School

WHY ME?

Each day they call me horrible names
As they refuse to let me play their games

I think about the nasty jeers and sneers
As I wipe away my watery tears

What had I done to them?
Why could I not join in?
Was it the colour of my skin?

But inside I'm the same as you
I wish you could see me as my family do.

Try and understand me fully
Be a good citizen please don't be a bully.

Felicity Cowdrey (11)
Horspath Primary School

MY MUMMY

M y mum is beautiful
U nderstanding
M ummy loves me.
M y mum is kind.
Y ou look beautiful.

Samuel Boyd (7)
Horspath Primary School

THE BULLY

The bully came up to me,
Started to call me names.
I wish I didn't have eyes to see,
What they were going to do to me.

They kicked and punched,
Pushed and shoved,
They looked at me with glee,
Their victim was me.

They pushed me on the floor,
I cried, they just did it even more.
It was getting worse,
They even stole my purse.

I struggled up and ran,
I went as fast as I could.
I ran down an alley,
The gang caught up,
Suddenly I recognised one, her name was Sally.

She reached out and tried to grab me.
She held me there up in the air against the wall,
I started to call, she let me go.
They ran away, letting me fall.
They knew I was beaten by the look on my face
Why did they pick on me?
Was it the colour of my face.

Clare Swan & Claire Lyne (11)
Horspath Primary School

WHAT'S WRONG WITH ME

I wonder what's wrong with me?
Is it I that's the problem?
I am afraid to go out alone,
Can't confide in any one.

I wonder what's wrong with me,
I think I have no friends,
There's no one to talk to,
I wonder if they want revenge.
Every night I cannot sleep,
Voices in my head saying no.

I wonder what's wrong with me,
There's nothing to say,
What's going to happen,
To me next day?
I take it out on other people,
I know it's not right so why?

I wonder what's wrong with me,
Am I the problem?
I've failed in my test,
Whatever comes next?

I wonder what's wrong with me,
The days are getting too long,
And if they see me crying,
They'll know I'm weak, not strong.

Morag Lamont (11) & Amy Feldman (10)
Horspath Primary School

WHY ME

All my friends deserted me,
Threatened by the bully, him.
If they weren't on *his* side,
His life would be pretty grim.

I didn't tell anyone,
A teacher nor my Mum,
My schoolwork got really bad,
The bullies found it fun.

It seemed like decades before they stopped,
It was only really a month or two,
I still long to hear the words,
I'm not picking on you.

When I see kids playing,
With a ball or kite in the park,
I wish I too could play with them,
Until the skies get dark.

So here is my explanation,
And here's what I'm going to do,
I'll hand the paper over,
I'll tell them that it's true.

When they've finished reading,
And then look up at me,
I'll offer them my friendship,
I won't bully them, though I should feel free.

On a scale from 1 to 10,
I'm feeling right down low,
I wonder if *you* are too,
I wonder if you know. . .

Amy Feldman (10)
Horspath Primary School

THE BULLY

I was the victim. They were the bullies.
They were swearing in my ears.
I was alone, miserable and scared.
It was like I was the challenger in a wrestling match
And He was the champion.
He came round the corner.
Then 2 or 3 boys kept beating me up.
One punch came in then another.
I was treated like a punchbag in a boxing match.
One day when I was bigger
I came past the boy that had beaten me up.
I said 'I am bigger and stronger now.'
The boy felt smaller.
I thought that I would beat him like he did to me.
But then I said to myself. I want to be a good citizen.
So I lent him a hand.

Alex Walton (10)
Horspath Primary School

HORRIFYING LIMERICKS

I was sleeping in my bedroom
When a vampire appeared in the gloom
I ran to the door
Then I saw
Him climbing into his tomb.

Harry Talboys (9)
Horspath Primary School

LIMERICKS

There was a boy called Billy the Kid
Who ate ten cream buns for a quid
They said 'Are you faint?'
He replied 'No I ain't
But I don't feel as well as I did.'

Edward Burton (8)
Horspath Primary School

JAGUAR

Jaguar Jaguar stalks her prey
She never lets it get away.
She rips it open and chucks away the bits
She never eats.
Jaguar Jaguar every day laze in her
beautiful way.
Jaguar Jaguar her fur so soft her black
spots are like coal.
Jaguar Jaguar her sharp teeth make her
roar sound so fierce
Jaguar Jaguar her claws so fast through
the leaves on the ground.
Jaguar Jaguar can see six times better
than humans but only at night.

                    Jaguar Jaguar

Carl Sketton (9)
Millbrook Primary School

I AM A DOG

I am a dog
I am stuck in an empty house
I have no food.
I have no water, no light, no warmth.

I am stuck in an empty house.

All the windows and doors are shut tight and locked
I bark and bark and bark.
No one hears me.
I hunt for food.
No use there is nothing.

I am stuck in an empty house.

I used to run and play in the park
Happy and free I was then.
I used to catch the ball.
I used to jump up at my Frisbee.
I used to chase cats and wander through woods.
But I can't now because I'm stuck in an empty house.
I can't run and play in the park
I can't be happy and free.
I can't catch my ball.
I can't jump up at my Frisbee.
I can't chase cats through woods.
I can't do anything but die.
Because I'm stuck in an empty house.

Katie Baker (10)
Millbrook Primary School

SPRING POEM

Spring is coming, spring is coming
So is everything
Daffodils shining in the sun.
Birds sit and sing.

Spring is coming, spring is coming
Blossom on the tree.
Daffodils and snowdrops
Is it time for tea?

Spring is coming, spring is coming
And our Easter holiday
Two weeks off school
I think I might go out today.

Stephanie Newing (10)
Millbrook Primary School

SLOTH

The sloth moves slowly.
Slowly sliding towards the jungle
Slumbering in the amazon,
Staying as still as a store.
Soft smooth fur.
Slowly sliding towards the jungle.
Sleeping still.
Slowly moving to another branch,
Sleeping like a log
Nearly all day.
Slowly sliding towards the jungle.
Slowly moving in the sunlight,
Slowly drifting off to sleep.

Peter Nennstiel (9)
Millbrook Primary School

SPRING IS COMING

Spring is coming, spring is coming.
Blossom on the trees.
Each doing their best.
Spurting out new leaves.

Spring is coming, spring is coming
Each and everywhere.
Daffodils, tulips and snowdrops
Coming out over there.

Spring is coming, spring is coming
Easter eggs are there.
Chicks are being born.
As joy is everywhere.

Kira Martin (10)
Millbrook Primary School

SPRING IS COMING

Spring is coming, spring is coming
All the flowers and bees come out
Buzzing and woving in the spring
All the children run about

Spring is coming, spring is coming
All the eggs are cracking
We are going on a faster holiday
We have been packing

Spring is coming, spring is coming
All the daffodils everywhere
Baby birds are flying around
High in the spring air.

Charlene Breakspear (9)
Millbrook Primary School

I Am A Lion

I am a lion
I am caught in a cage
I used to roam like a king
Roar like thunder
And rest in hot places.

But I am caught in a cage.

Up I jump
And my head hits the metal bars
My solid brown claws scratch
But nothing happens
All these humans looking at me
And I can't do anything

But I am caught in a cage

I get a lousy slap of meat a day
But I've survived
Or ha . . .
They shot me because I was too old
So that's the end for me.

Jack Flanagan (10)
Millbrook Primary School

I Am A Monkey

I am a monkey
And I am stuck in a net
I used to swing from tree to tree
And play with my brothers and sisters
I used to tease the crocodiles
From up in the trees.
But I can't do that because

I am a monkey stuck in a net
Oh, no a man with a gun
He's going to shoot me with his gun and I will die
But I don't want to die
I want to swing in the trees
But in my amazement he set me free

And I am a monkey swinging in the trees.

Daniel Sayer (10)
Millbrook Primary School

I AM A DOLPHIN

I am a dolphin

I am stuck in a net.

I used to play around lots of children
I used to jump from side to side.
I used to play around with the fish.
I used; to hide away from the killer whale.

But now I'm stuck in a net.
I really hate it.
I wish I had my mum.

But now I can't play around with
lots of children.
I can't play around with the other fish.
I can't hide from the killer whales
because I'm dead.

Nicola Burgess (9)
Millbrook Primary School

I AM A RHINO

I am a rhino, trapped in a cage,
I mourn for my brother, two years older in age.
I used to charge at beetles.
Run and jump and hide,
For I am a rhino one that's lost its pride.

I am a rhino trapped in a cage,
I mourn for my brother, two years older in age.
All I can do now is sit down and wait,
While those nasty men out there decide my fate.

I am a rhino trapped in a cage,
I mourn for my brother, two years older in age,
I used to sit in the baking hot sun,
Chat and laugh with everyone,
But all I can do now is sit and wait
While those nasty men out there decide my fate.

Joe Jones (10)
Millbrook Primary School

THE SOUND COLLECTOR

The Sound Collector came this morning
With his big bag of sounds.
The scraping of the ice boots.
The sushing of the people.
The shivering of the throats.
And the booming of the speakers.
The Sound Collector left this morning
With his big bag of sounds.

Joel Taylor (9)
Millbrook Primary School

I'M A HYENA

I'm a hyena.
I'm stuck in an iron cage
I used to run in the shade
Dance around my prey.

But I'm stuck in an iron cage

I used to tear with my teeth,
Growl when anyone comes near me
And laugh at other animals.

But I'm stuck in an iron cage

I'm only waiting now
It's only a matter of time
Till death will come
Around me
And strike me down

The other animals are coming to look
And tease me

I'm still stuck in my iron cage

Suddenly the animals run
Along comes a car
A long thin man
And a deadly gun

Will they use it on me?

Joseph Colliass (10)
Millbrook Primary School

I Am A Lion

I am a lion
I am stuck in a circus
I used to relax in the shade
But not any more
I used to relax in the shade whilst
The lionesses go and catch food
But not any more
I am stuck in a circus
I used to run about and play with friends
I used to roar when I yawn
But not any more
I am stuck in a circus
All I can see now is eyes watching me
And other animals locked up like me.

James Bowsher (10)
Millbrook Primary School

I Am A Bee

I am a bee
Stuck in a honey jar
I used to buzz around, buzz off
Buzz in and out
I used to buzz around picnics
And scare little girls
I used to visit flowers and drink their nectar
I used to make honey
But now I'm stuck in a honey jar waiting to die.

Matthew Burgess (10)
Millbrook Primary School

I AM A MONKEY

I am a monkey stuck in a tree
My mummy told me it was too high for me.

I used to drink water from the water hole.

I am a monkey stuck in a tree
My mummy told me it was too high for me.

I would go and pick nuts and fruit
And of course berries too.

I am a monkey stuck in a tree
My mummy told me it was too high for me.

I slipped and barely caught a
            branch running after my brother.

I hate him I really, really do.
Please set me free.

Daniel Aspell (9)
Millbrook Primary School

SNAKE

The snaky sound of the anaconda
Slithering, hissing, along the slidy ground
Swerving, swinging, swooping, swallowing
the insects at the swamp surface
Slinky, slowly slivers across the forest floor,
Stooping slowly, slimy slivers it's way home.

Mark Johnstone (10)
Millbrook Primary School

THE SILENT GHOST

Swiftly, silently along the hall,
A shadow moves, who can it be?
The silent ghost comes down the stairs,
Swiftly, silently as she moves.
She won't say a word,
Crying silently for herself.
No one noticing if she's there.
Midnight strikes.
She quickly runs
To the clock where she belongs.
She climbs in
Never comes out
Because nobody cares.

Laura Adams (9)
Our Lady's Convent Junior School

A CALCULATOR

Tap the buttons one, two, three.
Tap! Tap! Tap!
Tap the buttons endlessly.
Tap! Tap! Tap!
Addition and subtraction,
Tap! Tap! Tap!
Multiplication and division,
Tap! Tap! Tap!
It's easier than in your head
Tap! Tap! Tap!
So use your calculator instead
Tap! Tap! Tap!

Sophie Haverton (10)
Our Lady's Convent Junior School

SPACE POEM

Space shuttle,
5, 4, 3, 2, 1.
Blast-off,
The space the darkness,
The nothing,
Planets.
Mercury, Venus,
Earth, Mars,
Jupiter, Saturn,
Uranus, Neptune,
Pluto the last planet.
What will the space shuttle come to next?
Undiscovered planets desolate, empty,
Aliens!
Blast-off,
Touch down in Kennedy Space centre.

Richard King (11)
Our Lady's Convent Junior School

A BLEAK DAY

As I look to the sky
Rain drops falling from on high,
Cold and wet, damp and bleak,
Garden stretches on and on
Where we play hide and seek.
Oh I wish the sun would peep out and hiss,
'Go away clouds, dry up the rain
And see us playing once again!'

Katy Cave (10)
Our Lady's Convent Junior School

MY DOG

My dog is a bonny black thing,
He likes his food, and chews on a ring.
Outside we run and play,
Inside we will not stay.

He plays with the horses and the cats.
He also has his favourite mat.
His favourite food is a juicy bone,
He chews them like an ice-cream cone.

He plays with everyone.
He watches out for anyone,
Who happens to be humming,
And barks at them when coming.

Olga Luscombe (10)
Our Lady's Convent Junior School

CLOUDS

I dreamed of a cloud
With me on top shouting loud
All white and fluffy
Bouncy and puffy
Travelling over Earth
Seeing people digging turf
Falling off the cloud
With my mum shouting loud
Landing in bed
White and fluffy
Bouncy and puffy.

Felicity Coles (9)
Our Lady's Convent Junior School

THERE'S A CAT ON THE . . . .

There's a cat on the wall
Which comes here every day
It's black and white and small
And never stays away.

There's a cat on the chair
which nibbles at a sock
He loves to scratch and stare
And he'd look funny in a frock.

There's a cat on the rug
He tangles himself in string
I think he's very snug,
And he loves a big sponge ring.

Philippa Smith (10)
Our Lady's Convent Junior School

CELEBRATION 2000

I'm going to celebrate the millennium
On New Year's Eve this year
I'm going to drink fizzy pop
My dad will have a beer.

We are having a real big party,
My mum will drink champagne
There will be loads of spicy food
But I think I'll have something plain.

At midnight we'll turn the TV on
And listen to Big Ben chime
We'll pull our party poppers
And then sing Auld Lang Syne.

Ben Green (9)
Our Lady's Convent Junior School

MY HAMSTER

It's soft and small.
It's sweet and cuddly
It fills up its pouches
And I bet you don't know what it is . . .

It likes to bury.
It likes its food.
It likes to run through its exercise tube,

And I bet you don't know what it is . . .

She's as warm as a flame
She's as wriggly as a worm,
She's my sweet pet
And I bet you don't know what it is . . .

It's my hamster warm and cuddly.

Laura Dziewulski (9)
Our Lady's Convent Junior School

SOLAR SYSTEM

Sun, the fiery ball energising all life,
Mercury, near the sun,
Venus, next in line,
Earth, human being land,
Mars, the red planet,
Asteroid belt, balls of rock flying,
Jupiter, the biggest boss,
Uranus, blue lights flash,
Neptune, multicoloured beauty,
Pluto, cold freezer,
Beyond this who knows.

Matthew Gottwald (11)
Our Lady's Convent Junior School

MY FAVOURITE TOY

My favourite toy's a rag doll,
I love her very much
My rag doll's falling to pieces
I still love her very much.

She has a checked dress,
And matching shoes.
She is on the bed at night time,
And I cuddle her all night long.

My favourite toy's a rag doll
I love her very much
My rag doll will be with me,
Into the year 2000 and beyond.

Hannah Sarsfield-Hall (8)
Our Lady's Convent Junior School

FLOWERS

I love flowers they smell so sweet
In the spring there are lots to meet
Daffodils, tulips or maybe posies
Buttercups, daisies or even roses.

Some are still buds
And can't be seen
Most of them are different colours
Of red, blue and green.

On the field I'm making daisy chains
While everyone else is running in their lanes
I love flowers now you see
The person that loves flowers is truly me.

Nicola Mansell (9)
Our Lady's Convent Junior School

SPACE

Big with sea and land,
Earth has mountains and sands.

Producing heat and light
The sun is hot and very bright.

Twinkling in the night sky
Stars are way up high.

Many people wish to visit Mars
Pluto, Jupiter, Uranus and the stars.

There are comets with their trail
Rockets go up with a silvery tail.

Imogen Maund (10)
Our Lady's Convent Junior School

TO THE MOON

Five, four, three, two, one lift off.

The roaring of the rockets,
Shakes tools in my pockets.

A G-force of five,
Will I stay alive.

Up, up and away,
I've trained years for this day.

The Earth a little ball,
Becoming so so small.

Dials to check buttons to press,
This is making loneliness.

William Peskett (10)
Our Lady's Convent Junior School

BEANIE BABIES

I love my little Beanie Babies,
Soft as soft can be.
They all have different birthdays
And mean a lot to me.

There are lots of types of animals
Like snakes, cats, dogs and rabbits.
They are all so cute and cuddly
And don't have dirty habits!

My favourite Beanies are the bears.
They are the cutest of them all.
There's Britannia, Valentino, Princess and Fortune.
I hang them on my wall.

I wonder if there will be a millennium bear
To celebrate 1000 years.
Born on January 1st year 2000
Collectors will give 3 cheers!

Hayley Bater (8)
Our Lady's Convent Junior School

SPRING

Look, the winter has passed
The rain is over and gone.
I see the blossoms appearing in all the land.
The time has come for the birds to sing
Like the cooing of doves we hear in our land.

Emily Owen (8)
Our Lady's Convent Junior School

WHERE I LIVE

I have a cottage with a thatched roof
A garden that is green
A stable with a pony
Where I live is like a dream

Nice clean country air
Some pretty flowers and trees
A quiet and gentle breeze
Where I live has all of these

A frisky little lamb
A dashing little stream
The wail of distant hunters horns
Where I live is like a dream

Where I live is very pretty
It seems to go for miles
It spreads across the country
Where the sun smiles all the while

Gemma Allen (10)
Our Lady's Convent Junior School

MY FRIEND

Little freckles upon her face,
Short brown hair.
She's as bouncy as a bouncy ball,
Keeping still she cannot bear.

Lively, kind, greeny-brown eyes,
She's an understanding girl.
She tells funny jokes
That make my toes curl.

Victoria Barclay (9)
Our Lady's Convent Junior School

UP ON THE FARM

Up on the farm there are lambs being born,
Some are black, some are white
And some are black with white spots
Some are big, some are small.

When the lamb is born a bag comes out of the mother,
Then a lamb pops out and
The mother licks it.

If the lamb is too small it goes into
Something called a warming box
A warming box is a box with
Hay in, and a light on the top to
Keep the lambs warm.

Some mother sheep do not have any milk in their
Udders.
Some sheep have one lamb,
Some have two,
Some clever sheep have three.

After a day or two,
The farmer puts rings on their tails
So their tails drop off.
Then they will not get dirty tails,
I love the lambs.

Jessica Harris (8)
Our Lady's Convent Junior School

MY PUPPET

Puppet Pat is a clown,
When I let go he falls down

When I am in bed his
Nose is glowing red.

My puppet's mouth goes up
And down when you pull the strings.

He dances just like you and me.

His smile cheers you up
When you are down in the dumps.

If you move the right strings he will give you
A jolly jig.

If you ever see puppet Pat
Give him a wave and he will wave back.

Niamh Cahill (9)
Our Lady's Convent Junior School

DAY AND NIGHT

The sun and the moon come and go,
Day brings happiness and joy.
The sun brings blossom and daffodils,
And birds who sing all day long,
And beautiful butterflies that fly,
Ant scatter about all day long in the fly traps.
Night comes, ants are asleep and out
Come the vampire bats
To feed on animals blood, like every night.
Day comes.

Kimberley Agostino (8)
South Moreton Primary School

WINTER AND SUMMER

Wet winter has turned the hot sun into a
White sheet across the ground.
Winter has turned summer around.
Winter is cold, winter is white, winter is very, very bright.
Winter comes, winter goes, winter is cold between your toes.
Winter's gone, summer's here, we are travelling
Through the year.
Summer's hot, bright and bold, summer's something
To behold.
Summer's green like never you've seen,
It's as strong as a laser beam.
Winter and summer have gone, this year we will wait
Until next time they're here.

Jeremy Stockdale (8)
South Moreton Primary School

SPRING

Spring is the time we all love,
Spring is the time when in the tree sits the lovely white dove.
Spring greets you with birds singing in the trees,
Spring is the time with the blossom and the bees.
Spring is the time that we all play,
Spring is the time with a wonderful day.
In the year comes spring, spring is a special and a
wonderful thing.

Spring is the time when I should say 'I love you'.

Carmela Liverton (8)
South Moreton Primary School

SPRING AND AUTUMN

The trickle of water, the crunch of leaves,
autumn has come, we'll have some fun!
Soft and bright, gallons of light,
it's changeable and cloudy anything you like.
The crunch of leaves like a bag of crisps,
colours of all kinds like pots of paints.
Autumn comes, autumn goes,
the crunch of leaves under your toes.

Spring has come, lambs have fun,
hooray what a day!
Spring is here it's another year,
it's jolly and happy, bunnies play.
Now the crunchy, colourful leaves are gone
and the jolly, happy spring.
Come back next year!

Ben Hordienko (8)
South Moreton Primary School

AUTUMN AND SPRING

Autumn is when the leaves change colour
Autumn is when the leaves float off the trees
Autumn is fun
Spring is when blossom grows on trees
Spring smells of flowers
Spring is colourful
Spring is breezy, cool
Spring is sunny.

Katherine Murphy (7)
South Moreton Primary School

WINTER

Winter comes with its icy blasts,
Cuddled up, warm and indoors at last.
The snow outside softly falls,
Deep and inviting it calls.

Christmas Eve at last arrives,
Shoppers busy like bees in their hives.
Children tucked up, warm in their beds,
Will St Nick bring a new ted?

I love the winter's wonderland,
With its cool, crisp mornings and frost all around.
But very soon the green grass will appear,
Spring will come, summer's near.

Alex Cracknell (8)
South Moreton Primary School

LAND AND SEA

Small and not very tall
Rubbish spoils it too
Cleaning it that's what I do
Wet, sloppy and sometimes choppy
Is the sea
As wet as can be
Wet sea, wet sea
Wet as wet as can be.

Ben Gummery (8)
South Moreton Primary School

DAY AND NIGHT

One dark starry night
Up in the gloomy attic.
I watch the stars
Make pictures.
I was really relaxed
And dreamy.
I wonder why they call night spooky.
I lay in my bed
And think about night
Until morning.
I woke up bright and early.
I feel the hot bright blue sky.
I faintly hear the children laughing.
I ran down the stairs,
Out of the door
And feel the excitement.
Bees look around
And see the lovely flowers outside.
I feel like I am going to have a nice day.
I skip and I see the bright shiny sun.
Birds, busy laying eggs,
Birds singing.
People like a bunch of smiling flowers.
I feel a nice breeze around me.

Zoe Shuttleworth (7)
South Moreton Primary School

WINTER

Fire crackling stockings hanging nearby
Children wishing time would fly
Father Christmas coming, Christmas treats
Hooray, hooray I've got treats look mum and dad
I've got treats
You are as lucky as can be
Our son.

Kerry-Anne Vaughan (8)
South Moreton Primary School

THE SPRING

The sun shines bright on the leaves.
The wind is blowing hard on the trees.
Mist fills the windows covering them all.
It is dark, gloomy and cold.
The trees shake the brown-green-yellow leaves off.
Leaves going green on the trees.

Alice Maddox (8)
South Moreton Primary School

ORANGE AND YELLOW

Orange glows like a goldfish,
Yellow's much like the sun.
Orange is friendly forever happy,
Yellow's quite much fun.
Orange is cheerful,
Yellow's smells like sweet perfume.
Orange, yellow, orange, yellow,
Orange and yellow.

Jocelyn Earl (8)
South Moreton Primary School

WINTER

Winter has come, swallows have gone,
Time to begin the fun.
Make the snowmen,
Play on the logs, icy ponds where the fishes are.
Hard to breathe in the cold air as the wind blows,
Robins' feathers blow up to keep them warm.

As the snow falls,
It goes on your toes and gets them cold.
All different colours on the log
Like lollipops.
As the different colours fade away,
And you can take the ice off the logs, the green will come off.
If you can play football in the frost
You will slip over and get a wet bottom.
When you leave your football out in the garden
It will get snow on,
Cold and slippery it might get hard ice on it
Which you will have to run hot water over it.

Ruth Wollen (8)
South Moreton Primary School

THE SUMMER

The summer has come,
The spring is behind,
And the leaves
Are growing again.
People in their swimming pools
Dressing up in shorts and T-shirts.
The people are sweating in the sun.

Nathan Butler (9)
South Moreton Primary School

SUMMER AND WINTER

The summer is hot
The winter is cold
The summer is yellow
The winter is icy
The summer is singing
The winter is gone
The summer is love.

James Lineker (7)
South Moreton Primary School

WATER

Water is wet but can be ice,
Water is clear but can be blue,
Water can be sparkly or dull,
Water is cold but can be hot.

Nathan Randall (8)
South Moreton Primary School

THE NIGHT SECRETS

The moon is up
The stars are up too.
The moon is white as snow
The stars are gold as a gold statue.
The moon has a face, the stars have not.
I like the moon and the stars.
Which do you like best?

Amy Burkett (8)
South Moreton Primary School

SPRING AND AUTUMN

On warm spring mornings I feel so fresh
And new,
Daffodils are swaying in the grass and dew,
Spring and autumn,
Are so pretty just like me and you.
Sometimes I look at the sky,
When the grass is dry.
Spring and autumn,
Always love us,
Spring and autumn,
Spring and autumn . . .

Nicholas Redding (8)
South Moreton Primary School

SPRING

The spring has come
The blossoms grow and the winds blow.
The lambs are like snow
That glows.
The leaves start growing
From the happy buds.
The fresh air blows
And the blue sky glows.
The warm grass shines
Like the birds' rhymes.

Paige Mace (8)
South Moreton Primary School

BLACK AND WHITE

Black and white
Black and white.
White is the colour of my bedroom.
Black is the colour of the sky when
The bats fly by in the dark, dark sky.
White is the colour of the lambs playing in the meadows.
Black is the colour of ink and white goes with anything.
Black is dull.
Black and white together make a bowl.

Georgia Manning (8)
South Moreton Primary School

SPRING

When spring has come we see the sun and the
Breeze is blowing slowly.
The lambs are running and the blossom is
Swaying on the trees.
The flowers are growing
And the bees are buzzing away,
And its such a nice day to play.

Peyton Squires (8)
South Moreton Primary School

SNAKES

Snakes move with grace
And dignity
They move with s's and
Coils
They slither and slink
Through the world

Snakes all have different
Habitats
They like dark holes
And decorate trees
Like necklaces and bangles
There are even snakes in deserts!

Snakes have amazing colours
Myriad colours of the
Rainbow
Their skin can be zigzagged
Spotted, striped or plain

Poisonous and harmless
Snakes
All have glittering, needle
Fangs
And flickering black forked
Tongues

Snakes sparkle, slither
And squirm
In and out of bushes, shrubs
And trees
A flash of yellow
A glimpse of black

Large snakes, small snakes
A zigzag in the desert
In colours, designs and
Lengths
All snakes are unique.

Becky Sage (9)
The Manor Preparatory School

DEATH IN THE AFTERNOON

An unmoving coil of red and black
Sleeping in the afternoon sun.
Its evil unblinking eye surveying its territory
Slowly, its diamond shaped head rears up.
A forked tongue tastes the air.
Noiselessly, it slithers on its belly through the long grass.

Swiftly gliding over the ground,
Suddenly it stops,
It strikes,
Darting tongue,
Venomous fangs,
Wide-open mouth,
Swallowing whole,
The frog was gone.

Frances Rose (8)
The Manor Preparatory School

SNAKES

Snakes shiny and looking slimy
Slithering through dark, damp places
Sliding from side to side
Slipping away after plopping into water.

Snakes hissing with cruelty
Staring always, their eyes never blinking
Shining fangs dripping with venom
Swallowing prey whole.

I like snakes.

Helen Miller (9)
The Manor Preparatory School

PARTY RAP

In the streets there's lots of noise,
Made by the excited girls and boys.
    Let's party, let's party!
Look at the children having fun,
Laughter shared by everyone.
    Let's party, let's party!
Fireworks brighten up the sky,
Celebrations have soon gone by!
    Let's party, let's party!
It's the year 2000!
I'm not staying at home,
I'm going to visit the Millennium Dome!

Stacey Ollenbuttel (10)
Thomas Reade CP School

MILLENNIUM, MILLENNIUM

The Dome is being built,
A turtle on metal stilts.

The world went bang,
And the celebration began,
Millennium, millennium.

Time capsule in the ground,
Will '81 be found?

The world went bang,
And the celebration began,
Millennium, millennium.

Fireworks, robots and a hol-i-day,
Everyone celebrate the world's birthday.

The world went bang,
And the celebration began,
Millennium, millennium.

New technology all around,
To the space station we are bound.

The world went bang,
And the celebration began,
Millennium, millennium.

2000 years just went by,
But we still ask ourselves . . . why?

Peter Mulholland (11)
Thomas Reade CP School

Techno 2000

Fireworks and celebrations
Millennium Dome and jubilations
Microchips, computers too
Lots of things for you to do

2000, 2000 is the year
Auld Langs Syne and lots of cheer

Time capsules and a new space station
Hifi system, what a sensation
Computer chips and computer bugs
Could new technology pull the plugs?

2000, 2000 is the year
Auld Langs Syne and lots of cheer

Old technology in the bin
New technology is coming in
As the year is closing in
Let's have a party and make a din.

Daniel Thomas (10)
Thomas Reade CP School

Bugs

The computer bug is bugging around.
New technology is running about.
Computers crashing all year round.
In the future there will be, new computers for us to see.
Out with the old and in with the new.
There's something for all of you.

David Tyler (11)
Thomas Reade CP School

MILLENNIUM 2000

Open your eyes, look around you,
2000 is twelve strikes away,
What did you and your family do?
Did you have fun on the way?
Look back to the 20th century.

Open your eyes, look around you,
The places that you'll visit,
The new things that you'll see,
It's only a matter of waiting,
But I'm excited and worried also.

Open your eyes, look around you,
People all alone,
Nobody beside them for the millennium,
Their wish is that it never comes.

James Doman (10)
Thomas Reade CP School

CELEBRATION 2000!

5, 4, 3, 2, 1
Happy millennium
Fireworks and laser displays filled the sky
They screamed and popped.

Banged and hopped
Across the black waves of darkness.

Goodbye 1999, hello 2000!

Gary Lands (11)
Thomas Reade CP School

CELEBRATION 2000

Parties
Parades all over the world
Celebrating 2000
People all over the world will live
In happiness
Fireworks explode into beautiful colours
The colours will go into the sunset above the horizon
New pop groups, new shops, new films, new fashions
Will burst into your mind
The Millennium Dome will open
People will spill in to the millennium celebration.

Lucy Hill (11)
Thomas Reade CP School

WELCOME TO THE MILLENNIUM 2000

12 o'clock has gone
Fireworks sparkle in the sky
A new year, a new start
People celebrate
The Millennium Dome opens
Robbie Williams' song
Bubbly champagne goes pop
Everyone is ready to party
So new pop groups are ready to rock the world
The year 2000 is here
Enjoy yourself and make the best of it.

Emma Terry (11)
Thomas Reade CP School

HERE IT COMES, MILLENNIUM

It stands big and bold throughout the land
Built with the finest of hands
The Millennium Dome built with fun
Offers facilities to everyone

New ideas, new inventions
Come and ask lots of questions
Hands on
Why and when?
Celebrate the millennium

As I see the Dome being assembled
I think to myself what a wonderful symbol

In the year two thousand
Let's have fun
Love and peace to everyone.

Matt Walton (11)
Thomas Reade CP School

MILLENNIUM 2000

The fluorescent fireworks are here,
Lighting up this wonderful year.
The fireworks light up the dark sky,
My 'o' my the year's gone by.

Small rockets fly into the night sky,
They burst into thousands of fireballs.
Everyone dancing down below,
All the lights glow and glow.

It's the millennium!

Katie Hudson (10)
Thomas Reade CP School

Millennium 2000

Millennium fun this is a party for everyone.
Music, discos, would you please sit down,
have some Doritos.
Now it is here, celebrate the new year.
Jesus' birthday will now be celebrated.

Katie Hughes (10)
Thomas Reade CP School

Millennium

M illennium Bug,
I t will be here,
L ike a flash of lightning,
L ight up the fireworks,
E veryone drinks champagne and wine,
N ow you can hear the music,
N early year 2000,
I am having a celebration,
U nblock your ears, get ready for the singing,
M illennium is here, *finally!*

Simon Green (10)
Thomas Reade CP School

Millennium

When 12 o'clock comes, a new year begins
Everyone's ready to party.
There's bubbly champagne and fireworks too
So bring your friends and family.
This year is special, it's 2000
And the Dome is ready to rock.

Sapphire Parrott (10)
Thomas Reade CP School

THE TORNADO

The total destruction
made by its powerful force
It's very frightening
Winds over 100 mph
Roofs are lifted off homes
Cars sucked up and
tossed about
Its constant
spinning
can
up-root
trees
Its very
frightening
Deadly
twisters
very
frightening.

Jake Lynch (11)
Thomas Reade CP School

MILLENNIUM BUG

Will the digital watches flash 2000,
When the clock strikes 12.00?
Will everything go wrong?
The computers may stop working,
Whatever happens,
It will be an adventure for everyone.

Abigail Simpson (10)
Thomas Reade CP School

CELEBRATION

In the millennium the Dome may rule,
With its towers standing tall.
In the centre of Greenwich
In the centre of time.

It's a new
Year,
Decade,
Century or
Millennium.

There it was like a comet dashing round,
Frozen before crashing into the icy ground.
Next to the Dome,
In the centre of Greenwich,
In the centre of time.

It's a new
Year,
Decade,
Century or
Millennium!

Chris Hornsey (10)
Thomas Reade CP School

SNOW IS A WHITE CUB

Snow is a playful cub,
Pure and white,
Heavenly falling,
As the white lion plays,
Heavily laying down to sleep,
No sound is heard.

Fiona Alderman (11)
Thomas Reade CP School

MILLENNIUM

Happiness, laughter and fun
at the start of the year.
Millennium 2000 is right here.

Fairs and carnivals
hip hip hooray.
Parties and parades
carry on all day.

Fireworks burst and boom
at twelve o'clock.
People give presents to
make the hour rock.

The Millennium Dome
is open at last.
'Yippee!' 1999 has passed.

Katie Young (10)
Thomas Reade CP School

MILLENNIUM

The millennium has come,
The millennium is here.
The world will start again,
In a whole new year.
At 12 o'clock midnight
Children will cheer
And all the parents will drink lots and lots of beer.

Melissa Denton (10)
Thomas Reade CP School

MILLENNIUM DAWNING

The millennium is dawning,
It may be here in the morning.
The colourful fireworks are here,
Without noticing some dejected people are near.

People trying to squeeze past,
The year will pass at last.
The millennium will finally be here,
But it will take the world all year.
The sunset has passed and so has noon,
The darkness has risen and so has the moon.

Most people are celebrating about,
But some people could do without.
Sad people watching them all,
The happy people don't know at all.

Sarah Bruce (10)
Thomas Reade CP School

ACROSTIC 2000

M illennium has come, so party, disco and dance
I ndia, Japan, England, China, they'll all be celebrating
L earn from our elders and include the millennium
L earn, learn, learn, it's the best thing you can earn
E xciting isn't it or is it?
N ovember, December, now it's here
N ot many people get to see a new millennium
I t's here, it's here, now it's here
U nder utter moonlight it appears!
M illenniums are special, remember that!

Darryl Kelly (10)
Thomas Reade CP School

MILLENNIUM COUNTDOWN

Tick-tock, tick-tock goes the clock,
One minute till millennium.
Time is ticking away, ticking away.
50 seconds to go.

Some will be glad, some will be sad,
Some will not even know.
40 seconds to go.

Some will be partying, some will be working,
Some will just stay at home.
30 seconds to go.

Some will be waiting for the 'Bug',
Some will be sitting there with their mug.
20 seconds to go.

Who will be at the Dome?
People with money?
People with power?
But not the people who sleep in doorways
Instead of ivory towers.
10 seconds remain,
9, 8, 7, 6, 5, 4, 3, 2, 1

Happy millennium . . . everyone?

Robert Beasley (10)
Thomas Reade CP School

A NEW ERA

A brand new era is coming through
A celebration just for you
A new currency and quadraphonic sound
A jamboree all around.

Millennium Dome, Millennium Dome
I wanna make it . . . my home.

New technology and space stations
Peace and sincerity throughout the nations
Computer buddies, robot chums
That have real working lungs.

Millennium Dome, Millennium Dome
I wanna make it . . . my home.

Nick Quirk (10)
Thomas Reade CP School

THE YEAR 2000

M   illennium Bug *beware!*
  I   t'll scatter around until the next year.
e L   ectrical goods you're in for a scare.
  L   et's party until the lights go out.
  E   ven if that bugs about.
  N   ow uncover the capsule of BP.
  N   ever to be seen again.
  I   f only I could live.
  U   ntil the next
M   illennium.

Lewis Jones (10)
Thomas Reade CP School

WHEN I GO TO SECONDARY SCHOOL

When I go to secondary school
Everyone is bigger than me
I won't find my way around the school
For about three days

I am worried about the size of the big school
I am nervous about all the hard work and beastly homework
I am scared of the bullies that will pull my hair
I am frightened that horrible people will send
                    me to the wrong classroom

Going to a big school is very weird
There are lots of things going round in my head
It makes me feel dizzy
I can't concentrate
It makes me want to cry.

Shelley Baker (10)
Thomas Reade CP School

MILLENNIUM 2000

M illennium brings joy and happiness.
I   t will bring parties and happy, happy, joy, joy.
L ife will be fun with new things.
L ife is fun and joyful.
E venings are happy and joyful.
N othing will be the same.
N othing, I say nothing.
I   n the night it is dark.
U n do the night and see the
M illennium.

Jamie Morse (10)
Thomas Reade CP School

MILLENNIUM POEM

Robots, robots, robots galore
They're coming through the floor
To take over humanity
To civilise the world
Robots, robots, robots galore
No more humans any more.

Ashley Stables (10)
Thomas Reade CP School

ROBOTS

Beep, beep, beep
Robots rule
The human world
Everything is done by
Robots, robots, robots
A new generation
Of robots
Humans will no longer
Exist, exist, exist.

Charlotte Hooper (10)
Thomas Reade CP School

1000 YEARS

1000 years have passed since the last millennium,
1000 years to go until the next millennium,
I wish I could be there in the year 3000,
No more poverty, no more suffering, no more war,
That would be the perfect world,
It's a shame it won't be like that this year.

David Tompkins (11)
Thomas Reade CP School

THE DAY I FELL DOWN THE CHIMNEY

The day I fell down the chimney
Is a day I'll never forget,
I got all dirty and dusty,
It's the dirtiest I'll ever get!

I came falling and falling
Until I landed in a pit
And then I started calling,
Waiting there I sit.

After 10 minutes or so
I saw a long brown rope,
So I climbed up till half way
And then I suddenly stopped.

My foot slipped as I climbed up
And I came shooting down again
I fell right to the bottom
And it caused a lot of pain.

The day I fell down the chimney
Is a day I'll never forget,
I got all dirty and dusty
It's the dirtiest I'll ever get!

I wonder why I climbed up the chimney
In the first place,
I was only trying to be Santa for my little brother,
All because of my stupid shoe lace!

Hannah Jones (10)
Thomas Reade CP School

BUGGINESS

In the moonlight people are shouting 'Twelve!'
Old friends or relations perhaps,
They're having a pint in the public house,
It's nearly 12 o'clock.

Suddenly as the clock strikes twelve,
All the lights go out,
The beer machine goes crazy,
The Millennium Bug has hit.

TVs are flipping channels,
Videos won't work;
All the captured stars on sticks
Planted in the road go out.

The Internet goes wacky,
Video game systems go out,
E-mails are going weird,
The Millennium Bug is here.

What's happened to my PC?
It's going really weird;
Daddy, will you help me please?
The Millennium Bug is here.

Thomas Winwood (10)
Thomas Reade CP School

IT'S THE MILLENNIUM BUG

Bugs, bugs everywhere
In my computer, it's everywhere
They are in the garden under my shed
It's driving me crazy, it's getting to my head.

My computer's going wonky
Printers too
Lights went out at supper time
And my brother ate my stew.

Robbie Davis (10)
Thomas Reade CP School

Don't Change My Nappy

Run away from Mum,
Run away from Mum,
She'll put that cold cream on,
She'll blob it on and make me scream!
It's as cold as ice-cream,
She'll never catch me, I'm too fast,
That 'orrible cream really lasts,
I can feel it run down my nappy,
It don't make me very happy,
I'll stop her one day,
She'll never catch me,
But she's caught Lee,
Argggg!
Now it's me!

Charlotte Davies (11)
Thomas Reade CP School

THE PAST 2000 YEARS

2000 years gone by,
And since the year zero,
Many eras have passed,
And many still to go.

The Romans until now,
Have all had rich rulers,
Kings, queens and presidents,
Some countries had intruders.

Philip Platt (10)
Thomas Reade CP School

MILLENNIUM 2000

Millennium 2000
A historic mark in time,
A celebration for everyone,
Together all mankind,
Forget the feuds of the past,
Let all love and friendship last,
Let's all learn to live together,
From this moment in time, let us treasure,
The party's only just begun,
So let's *rock* this millennium.

Adam Jones (10)
Thomas Reade CP School

BATH TIME

I hate the bath it is always too . . .
Hot really hot
It's like going in a pool of lava
It steams like a sauna
Burning steaming like a volcano
Frizzling, swishing, twirling
Red-hot, red-hot
Bubbling, swooping
It's like a volcano
Steaming and burning
I don't want to go in
Please don't make me go in
Again!

Hannah Taylor (11)
Thomas Reade CP School

AS I STAND AND LOOK

There I look upon the hill as it sometimes
Catches my eye
It twinkles and shines all over the world
As it's way up in the sky.

All the colour beams down
It looks like a dot in the sky
And it gleams like a golden crown.

Then it slowly dies away
But remembers to come back the next day.

Kirsty Parrott (11)
Thomas Reade CP School

THE FRIENDSHIP

As the friendship comes floating in
showing us how to forgive each other,
'It's a time for love,' the captain said
and the ship bobs up and down.
Remember to live in the past, present and the future
the announcement was heard.
Remember to begin each day with helpfulness
and end each day in kindness.
So have a happy millennium
the captain called,
as the ship drifts away.

Jane Boreham (11)
Thomas Reade CP School

FRIENDSHIP

Friendship is aided by the tide of time
When you travel over rough, gusty seas
You must grab onto the sail
When pushed by the strong wind,
Sometimes your friendship bobs
And flows on the calm waters
The ship must stay together or it will fall apart and sink
Friendship is aided by the tide of time.

Emma Ealey (10)
Thomas Reade CP School

ON THE PLAIN

Every day I come here,
Every day I think the same,
I wonder what happens,
On the other side of the plain.

Sometimes I see children play,
Having lots of fun,
The fun I haven't had,
Life might change, I am still young.

When the days are shorter,
And the nights are long,
Sometimes I am still here,
To hear the bird's song.

Their world is not known to me,
Though I come here again and again,
I have to keep on guessing,
What's on the other side of the plain.

James Wartke-Dunbar (11)
Thomas Reade CP School

2000

End of one century
Beginning of another
Exciting times, new things
Parties, celebrations
Food and drinks
Celebrate 2000
Millennium comes
It's a start of another.

Phum Probets (10)
Thomas Reade CP School

SWIMMING

In the classroom
lining up
gathering coats.

In the coach
sitting quietly
for swimming.

In the changing rooms
getting changed for swimming
in the showers.

In the pool
where is everyone?
Underwater.

In the showers
getting changed
into our clothes.

On the coach
very noisy
the teachers say 'Be quiet.'

In the classroom
getting IT books
for computers.

Thomas Lloyd (10)
Uffington Primary School

THE SHIP OF LIFE

I am standing on the pier looking out to sea,
The waves are calm and gentle,
Representing a calm life.
In the distance,
A flashing light,
Representing my future job.
The sand laying on the shore,
Gets less, as I grow.
And there they are,
My troubles,
They are the groynes.
And the lights behind me,
Like a gazing audience.
And the angry sea lashes against the defensive rocks,
The sea is trying to carry me off.
I am standing on the pier looking to sea,
The waves are calm and gentle,
Representing a calm life.

Karen Cooper (11)
Uffington Primary School

SWIMMING

Swimming - Monday take our swimming kit
Swimming - on the bus, we're on our way
Swimming - we get changed in the changing room
Swimming - in the shower, it is cold
Swimming - mats in the water
Swimming - we get on the mats, I fall off in the deep end.

Martyn Fowler (9)
Uffington Primary School

DREAMING UNDER THE WHITE HORSE

I am standing on the white horse gazing at different
Fields, churches, houses, wildlife
I am gazing at the steep hills
I am dreaming that the white horse will come to life
I am staring at the big open area
Sheep wandering along the grass
I am wondering what would happen
If I fell down the overgrown hills
I am thinking about music that would fill this space
Slow, quiet and dreamy music
I am dreaming, dreaming under the white horse.

Tom Cracknell (10)
Uffington Primary School

DREAMING UNDER THE WHITE HORSE

I've been here for thousands of years
I've seen Roman battles and huge storms
If I was free I would ride to Hawaii
I'm never lonely because
people are always around me.
I've seen buildings come
and buildings go.
I'm never hungry because there's
a giant manger down below me.

Jack Tilling (9)
Uffington Primary School

A Dog Competition

Get the brushes out
Groom Rufus
Do his ears
Quick, can't be late
Fur nice and shining
Eyes sparkling
Get in the car
Oh no
We're going to be late
Don't *panic*
We are here
Oh no, it's our turn
Come on Rufus, yes we've finished
Let's hear the results
Rufus is the *winner*
Yes, yes
Panic, panic
Last session
Jump down, crawl through a tunnel
Up over the seesaw
Here we go again
Panic, panic
Yes, this dog is the *champion*
Wow, excellent Rufus
Rufus jumps up and licks my face
I open my eyes
Rufus is on my bed
Ah!
What a dream!

Jonathan Ambidge (10)
Uffington Primary School

ARE YOU THERE?

Are you there mum
it's time for school
or I'll be late?

Are you there bus
I'm off to school
for maths?

Are you there
pattern in the times table
at school?

Are you there
packet of crisps
in my school bag?

Are you there
pen for English
and pad?

Are you there
teacher to do lessons
are you there?

Are you there
Lunch box
so I can have lunch?

Are you there
PE kit and
trainers?

Are you there
CD for assembly
for music?

Are you there mum?
'Yes I am.'
'Good, now I can go home.'

Georgia Black (11)
Uffington Primary School

TOURNAMENT

Getting ready for the tournament:
Organising practices,
Getting kit ready.
I've been in lots of other matches.
Won some,
Lost some,
Drew some.
I'm looking for my boots because I've lost them.
Searching my house
Under the bed,
In my bootbag,
In the dog's bed,
In the cupboard.
I've found them! Underneath loads of clothes.
I'm ready now,
The tournament can begin!

Tom Cooper (11)
Uffington Primary School

WHERE'S EVERYONE?

Silent classrooms,
Deserted and still,
No lights flickering.

Silent hall,
Dark and quiet,
Not a child or teacher in sight.

Silent office,
Not a sound,
Where is Mrs Smith?

Silent kitchen,
No delicious smells
And no cooks cooking.

Silent library,
Even more silent
Than I've ever seen it before.

Silent computer room,
Not a click of a key
Or mouse.

Silent toilets,
Not a child
Hanging up their bag.

Silent playground,
Not a scream
Or thumping of running feet.

Silent field,
Not a smack of
A foot on a ball.

Silent silence
Helps me to think,
And remember the church service.

Georgie Baily (9)
Uffington Primary School

MY FIRST DAY AT SCHOOL

Where are Mummy and Daddy? I want them now,
why do I have to learn?
I hate school, I want my mummy.
English, I hate English,
can't I do some maths?
I really like it.
Hello, is anyone there?
Mrs Green, where have all the children gone?
Oh it's home time, time to see my mummy and daddy
and go and have my lunch.
What, what is this?
Why aren't Mummy and Daddy here?
Oh hello Sissy, where are Mummy and Daddy?
I want my lunch now.
It's not lunchtime, it's playtime,
soon you will be going back to learn.
No, no, no, no.

Jackie Watson (11)
Uffington Primary School

WHERE HAS EVERYBODY GONE?

No one in the school
No one on the bus
No one in the changing rooms
No one in the toilets
No one in the shower.

Where has everyone gone?

Are they in the school? *No!*
Are they on the bus? *No!*
Are they in the changing rooms? *No!*
Are they in the toilets? *No!*
Are they in the showers? *No!*

Where has everyone gone?

In the swimming pool
Doing the fun swim!

Dale Whitehorn (10)
Uffington Primary School

THE SHIP OF LIFE

I am standing on the sand looking out to sea
Looking at the boats that will carry me far in the life that I am in.
The groynes, the gateway to heaven gape before me.
A voice seems to say 'Your destiny lies before you.'
The voice says 'As long as you have been good and gently
The gateway to heaven will always be open to you.'
So when I die, heaven will be open to me. . .
And I will wave the life that I have had a last goodbye.

Robert Bowsher (11)
Uffington Primary School

SWIMMING

In the bus
Sitting quietly
Sitting.

In the changing room
Changing into swimming suits
Changing.

In the showers
Freezing water
Freezing.

In the pool
Swimming widths
Swimming.

In the pool
Under water
Under.

In the changing room
Dripping wet
Dripping.

In the bus
Screaming children
Screaming.

In the school
Fed up with waiting
Fed up.

Sarah Cooper (9)
Uffington Primary School

FIRST DAY AT SCHOOL

My mum stopped at a building,
it was a big building,
we all got out and went inside.
All these people were bustling about.
I went into a room, and hung my coat up,
my mum followed me.
We came to another room and I got greeted by
a teacher. My mum said 'Goodbye.'
I said 'Why goodbye?' But she had gone.
'Mum, Mum, please don't leave me,' but she had gone.
The teacher gave me a colouring sheet to colour in.
'I don't want to colour in the Three Little Pigs . . .
I want my mum!'
After that we had a play,
I felt small and lonely.
A girl came up to me, her name was Charlotte.
I stuck with Charlotte.
When we went back inside the teacher gave me a book to read,
'I want my mum!'
But I opened the book, 'But I can't read it!'
So I looked at the pictures instead.
Then she (the teacher) gave me another colouring sheet.
'*I want my mum!* I don't want to colour in Red Riding Hood.'
Just then my mum walked in and took me home.

Sophie Bowsher (11)
Uffington Primary School

SWIMMING

In the classroom
gathering up
coats and bags

In the bus
sitting noisily
waiting to go

In the changing room
changing into
costumes and hats

In the pool
swimming with
other people

In the changing room
dripping with
water

In the bus
noisy children
waiting to go

In school
hair still soaking
and dripping with water.

Charlotte Bond (9)
Uffington Primary School

WHERE'S EVERYONE?

In the classroom
lining up
ready to go on the coach.

In the coach
sitting silently
ready to go.

In the changing rooms
getting changed
everyone puts on their costumes.

In the showers
getting wet
jumping in the water.

In the pool
under the water
getting a brick.

In the pool
the whistle blows
everybody evacuates the pool.

In the cloakroom
getting dry
hovering in our towels.

In the coach
seatbelts on
seatbelts off.

In school
reading
it's three o'clock.

In the school
it's home time
at last.

Anita Preston (10)
Uffington Primary School

DREAMING UNDER THE WHITE HORSE

I glance longingly at the white horse
desiring to touch it
the wind
ferocious against my face.
I feel as if I'm going to be lifted up
and carried away
by the untamed fingers.
I look out over the hills far and wide
I feel safe up here,
safe and alone, just me.
The air whistles quietly
but then the silence is split apart by
the screeching and roaring wind
roaring through the manger.
The horse must have seen so many things
battles . . .
seasons . . .
wet and damp snow . . .
sleighers, sun
and heard
travellers
and the scouring of the white horse.

Michelle Gaffka (10)
Uffington Primary School

THE SCAREDY OWL

Once there was a scaredy owl
Who sat in his tree
Thinking how nice it would be not to be frightened of mice.

So the owl in the tree
Went to see a man in a house
About not being scared of a little grey mouse.

Now this owl was getting rather thin
For no mice he could eat for his din
So the owl looked for a place where he could eat
Worms and grubs not mice and shrubs.

When the owl found a place he ate and got quite fat
So he was put to bed with a cloth on his head.

Louise Goyder (9)
Wantage CE Junior School

THE RAINBOW

Red is like anger, peering at the sun,
Orange is a fruit that can be recognised,
Yellow is the happiness, beaming through our eyes,
Pink is the beauty of the early morning rose,
Green is the river, cold and bare,
Speeding wind that is running through your hair,
Purple is like the colour of the gem of death,
Blue is like the trickling of rainfall,
That sits at the end of the rainbow.

Claire Humberstone (9)
Wantage CE Junior School

I WANT TO DRAW!

I want to draw
a scared lion
doing weightlifting.

I want to draw
a spotty mouse
dancing to Boyzone.

I want to draw
a fat fly sitting
on a chair.

I want to draw
a spotty rabbit
running fast.

Samantha Forrester (10)
Wantage CE Junior School

EASTER BUNNY

The Easter Bunny comes in the night,
The Easter Bunny comes before Easter Sunday,
He gives you Easter eggs,
He hides the Easter eggs he gives you,
He is never seen in the night,
He lives in Easter Egg Land,
He lives in an egg-shaped house,
He's white and fluffy,
He's small and fat . . .
       The Easter Bunny.

Adam Kelly (9)
Wantage CE Junior School

OLD PRAISE SONG OF THE BEAR
(Inspired by Sotho (Northern Transvaal) poem, 'Old Praise Song Of The Crocodile')

His coat is like silk.
He likes to hunt,
Down in the water.
His shout can be heard,
Round the wood.
They enter a cave, in a suitable way.
Down in the river, he hunts his prey.
Catches his prey, and kills it today.
When he goes back to his cave,
He rips it apart,
And eats, in an ordinary way.
He comes back for a new fish,
Today.

Michael Burch (8)
Wantage CE Junior School

WONDERING MIRACLE

I wonder if someone is out there,
wonder just wonder if I could see them.
Wouldn't it be a miracle if I could fly?
Up, up, up above the world so high
I would fly.
I wonder if I could fly
out of danger, out of trouble.
That is what anybody would call a
        Miracle.

Coral Lumsden (10)
Wantage CE Junior School

THE THIRD-FLOOR BEDROOM
(Inspired by Chris Van Allsburg's 'Mysteries of Harris Burdick')

A feather falls,
A neck moves,
A chirp sounds,
And a bird flies away.
Wings stretching as wallpaper birds come to life.
You can feel the magic in the air,
The wind is blowing softly
As the bird flutters upon the chest of drawers.
She looks out of the window,
She is ready to fly!
With a shower of feathers she flies away,
A flapping of wings . . .
I wake up!
And see that the birds are back in place.
Everything is still.

Grace Webster (9)
Wantage CE Junior School

IF

If boots could talk,
If rats could fly,
If rabbits could swim,
If trees could talk,
If dogs could speak,
If lions could moo!
If bears could stand on two feet,
If snakes could ribbit,
If axes could put wood back together,
Then the world would be the strangest place.

Christopher Richards (9)
Wantage CE Junior School

PLAYGROUND SOUNDS

As I stood in the playground I heard many sounds.
Birds twittering as they circle their nest,
Chicks squawking as they crack open their shell.
Blackbird singing showing off his glory,
People whispering, sharing all their secrets.
Children running faster than a hare,
Trees swaying like they're dancing in the breeze.
Leaves whooshing everywhere around me,
Then everything falls dead,
Except a plane, snoring in its bed.
I walk closer to the road, and snap a twig,
I could hear cars, roaring and raging along,
Motorbikes zooming along,
A woman on a bicycle dinging her bell.
Then another plane swoops over humming in the air.
I turn around and slowly walk back,
Away from the playground of many sounds.

Rebecca Grant (11)
Wantage CE Junior School

CALL CAT

Call cat light - feet,
Call cat sharp - claw,
Call cat kill - mouse,
Call cat house - guard,
Call cat fish - eater,
Call cat nine - lives,
Call cat hunter,
Call cat purr - thing,
But better wait,
        Till you cross the garden.

Duncan Boyle (9)
Wantage CE Junior School

THROUGH THE WINDOW

Go and look out the window.
Maybe you'll see a path,
or a little green tree
or even a small boy playing ball.

Go and look out the window.
Although it's not sunny,
it may be breezy.
There might be a bee,
buzzing around.

Go and look out the window.
There might be a gaudy peacock,
or a furious tiger,
hiding in the grass.

Go and look out the window.
You might not see anything exciting,
but there'll be something!

Asger Jakobsen (9)
Wantage CE Junior School

IF

If I was a dragon, I'd live in Storyland,
Breathe fire on the knights,
Have matchsticks named after me (they'd be the leading brand!)

If anyone came into my cave,
There would be an immense fight,
All the knights would be bleeding,
And I would be weeping in the night.

Matthew Bridle (8)
Wantage CE Junior School

THE MAGIC BOOK

Go and open the magic book.
Maybe there will be a fierce lion,
a cute kitten, a funny bunny
or a flying pig.

Go and open the magic book.
Maybe a peacock mating.
Maybe some geese are migrating,
or giant wrestling,
or a cloud in a cloud.

Go and open the magic book.
If there's a crowd,
the people will pass.

Go and open the magic book.
Even if there's only the light shining.
Even if there's only the hollow tree.
Even if no one's there,
Go and open the magic book.
Please.

Jason Taylor (9)
Wantage CE Junior School

CALL MONKEY
(Inspired by 'Don't call alligator . . . ' by John Agard)

Call monkey champion swinger,
Call monkey banana eater
Call monkey thin one,
Call monkey car wrecker,
Call monkey two legs,
Call monkey squealer.

Thomas Burdett (8)
Wantage CE Junior School

FAMILY AND FRIENDS

Friends are great,
They help you make
Friendships that will last forever,
Helping, working always together.

Families are full of fun,
Sister, Brother, Dad and Mum
Helping here and helping there,
Until they have some time to spare.

Friends are needed in all sorts of ways
Hard to get on when they're away,
Without my friends I would be lost
My best friend is beyond true cost.

Families have the best of care,
When they're wanted they are there,
Without them it wouldn't be the same
So families' friendship must remain.

Felicity Purdom (9)
Wantage CE Junior School

CALL SHARK

Call shark fierce teeth,
Call shark big mouth,
Call shark triangular fin,
Call shark raggedy mouth,
Call shark big body,
Call shark black mouth,
Call shark slimy mouth.

Michael Davies (8)
Wantage CE Junior School

OLD PRAISE SONG OF THE KILLER WHALE

He swims here and there, eating fish,
He's the killer of the seas.
I am the killer whale!
I stalk the seas,
Killing everything I see
I rip up big things,
I battle sharks and sometimes win.
I finish a fight, blood goes up to the surface.
I am the laughing killer.
I am the killer of the seas!

Matthew Walsh (9)
Wantage CE Junior School

OLD PRAISE SONG OF THE LION
(Inspired by Sotho (Northern Transvaal) poem,
'Old Praise Song Of The Crocodile')

The lion is king of the jungle,
He roams around, chopping up the innocent,
Having lunch any time of the day,
Mostly eating antelopes,
It drags its food behind a tree,
It is the predator.
First he rips their skin off,
Then takes out their heart,
Watch out animals, hear he comes!
He lives in the African jungle.

Thomas Bolton (8)
Wantage CE Junior School

If

If I was a ferocious lion,
I would rule the jungle and charge at my prey.
And if I was a terrifying, camouflaged rattlesnake,
I would poison my life food, and rattle myself away.
If I was a really scary, biting shark,
I would swim through the oceans,
With a smile on my face,
And scare all the fishes away.
And if I was a scary, creepy, horrifying tarantula,
I would poison everyone who walks in my way.

David Wells (9)
Wantage CE Junior School

Anger

Anger is like King Herod when Jesus was born.
Anger is like people dying.
Anger is like the pain of the years.
Anger is like the world being mean.

Tilly Hickman (8)
Wantage CE Junior School

Blue

Blue is like the midday sun,
Blue is like the falling rain,
Blue is like the river of pain,
Blue is like the ocean's depths.

Oliver Highton (9)
Wantage CE Junior School

THE GARDEN PATH

Go down the garden path.
Maybe you'll see a vivid peacock,
with a lot of bright staring eyes.
Maybe you'll see your future,
unfold in front of your very eyes.

Go down the garden path.
Achieve your destiny.
Look down the garden path,
go on the hot air balloon.

Go down the garden path.
Feel as free as a swooping dove.
Climb up the picturesque cherry tree.

If you go down the garden path,
you will always have time for tea.

Jordan Shoesmith (9)
Wantage CE Junior School

UNDER THE RUG

(Inspired by the work of Chris Van Allsburg's
'The Mysteries of Harris Burdick')

Shadows creeping on the side,
A big bump on the floor.
Three pictures on the forgotten wall,
A table lamp crashing 'pon the floor.
There's something hiding under the rug.

Jessica Stanton (9)
Wantage CE Junior School

PLAYGROUND SOUNDS

As I walked into the playground,
All I could hear was silence,
As if it had conquered the world,
But then I listened harder,
I heard lots of sounds like:
The twittering of a blackbird,
As it hopped from branch to branch,
The squeaking of the cars,
As they brake to stop.
The booming of the Concorde,
It was just like thunder.
The croaky coughing of Chris,
As he writes his poem.
The rush of the wind,
As it races through the newly flowered tulips
Wishing it could win
And last but not least,
The stomping of the feet,
As we go back to our classroom.

Danielle Langley (10)
Wantage CE Junior School

CALL ELEPHANT
(Inspired by 'Don't Call Alligator . . . ' by John Agard

Call elephant gray one,
Call elephant long nose,
Call elephant big tusk,
Call elephant giant feet,
Call elephant big body,
Call elephant loud mouth.

Celia Coules (9)
Wantage CE Junior School

WAKE UP

Wake up! Wake up! Today is light.
Get up! Get up! With all your might.
Get up my sweet, it's morning time.
If you wake up the sun will shine.

Today you will learn,
get up it's now your turn.
Now go outside,
or else you'll be tied,
at home all day.

Wake up! Please wake up!
Night has gone away,
today you will be strong
tomorrow you will be stronger.
So wake up! Rise and shine.
Yesterday has gone and light is present.
Wake up, little one.

Rachel Quinn (9)
Wantage CE Junior School

ANOTHER PLACE AND ANOTHER TIME
(Inspired by the work of Chris Van Allsburg's 'The Mysteries of Harris Burdick')

For little children on the rusty track,
There they go to the foolish, spiteful devil
Devil's house with skeletons being nasty,
Ghosts and bats flickering in the twilight,
If you go there,
You'll never live.

Amy Anderson (9)
Wantage CE Junior School

PLAYGROUND SOUNDS

A cloudy grey day
no wind,
standing in the playground
listening,
scurrying, hurrying pitter-pattering
feet,
echoing voices ringing round
the playground,
chit-chattering birds perching
on branches,
cawing crows flew up high
in the sky,
a van roared into the cheery
playground,
the bell goes and people
trudge in,

sudden silence.

Rhianna Drury (11)
Wantage CE Junior School

I ASKED A LITTLE BOY

I asked a little boy who cannot see,
What is colour like?
Why gold is like mine and Chloe's hair,
Green is like a little tiny weed, coming out of its bud,
Like some bright green grass.
Black is like the darkness of the night,
Red is like the devil's rough skin,
Yellow is like the sun beaming down,
Green is like the bright leaves, just growing.

Abbie Carter (8)
Wantage CE Junior School

GO AND OPEN THE FIRE EXIT

Go and open the fire exit,
you might see a magic city
a wonderland of a wonderland.

Go and open the fire exit,
you will see a land of clocks
many shapes and sizes.

Go and open the fire exit,
maybe you will see a walking cloud,
with a rumble.

Go and open the fire exit,
you might see a hard dragon
with sharp eyes.

Go and open the fire exit,
there might be a never-ending kind of a land
a city to end my poem.

Luke Faircloth (8)
Wantage CE Junior School

DEATH

Death is like the devil's pride,
Death is like nothing is there,
Death is like the world has stopped,
Death is like we are fading away,
Death is like the pain has gone,
Death is like the coffin's smell,
Death is like the stopping of the heart,
Death is like the devil's dinner,
Death is like the end of happiness.

Kerry Meaney (9)
Wantage CE Junior School

PLAYGROUND SOUNDS

As I stood in the playground I heard,
The chattering and chirping of birds,
The trees swinging in the breeze,
People laughing and shouting out words.

Cars screeching while going past,
A Concorde rumbling fast,
Planes vibrating, clamouring and roaring,
Pencil squeaking while writing and drawing.

Trees scraping like chalk on a blackboard,
An aerial on the car swishes and the engine roared,
Then silence,
That is what I heard in the playground.

Jennifer Day (10)
Wantage CE Junior School

IF

If there was no music,
No joy could happen.
If there were no trombones,
Sound would never be loud.
If there were no cellos,
Dvorak would be sacked.
If pianos weren't in the world,
Music would never come alive.
If violins never sounded,
Happiness could never happen.

Christopher Terepin (8)
Wantage CE Junior School

THE WINDOW

Go look out the window,
you never know what you'll see.
Go look out the window,
you might see the rushing blue sea.

Go look out the window,
you might see a dancing black bear.
Go look out the window,
you might see an elephant there.

Go look out the window,
you see a hollering ghost.
Go look out the window,
you could be surprised by burnt toast.

Go look out the window,
you don't know what you're missing.
Go look out the window,
Go on look!

Joanne Philp (9)
Wantage CE Junior School

MY PAPERWEIGHT IS LIKE

Raindrops, stopped before they end their life,
A rainbow floating into darkness,
A family come together
Planets in the non-understandable universe
The future of technology
The world coming to a steady stop
Something we don't understand.

Joanna Fox (9)
Wantage CE Junior School

PLAYGROUND SOUNDS

The blackbird sweetly chatting,
Calling the birds up high.
The plane engines roaring,
Across the moonlit sky.
The cars droning,
Then halting to a squeak.
The other children whispering,
Or being oblique.
The ants slowly crawling,
Across the mown lawn.
The leaves from the tree,
Falling to the floor.
The wind to my ear,
Like the sound of the sea.
These are all sounds,
From Wantage C of E.

Noori Brifcani (11)
Wantage CE Junior School

AERIEL

(Inspired by Shakespeare's 'The Tempest')

She moves rapidly through the morning air,
Blending into the cool sky,
When she does not want to be seen,
Made from a spell,
By Prospero's wizardry.
She is made out of a fraction,
Of cool air,
And moves on into the cloudy, morning sky.

Peter Berrett (8)
Wantage CE Junior School

MR LINDEN'S LIBRARY
(Inspired by the work of Chris Van Allsburg's 'The Mysteries of Harris Burdick')

A poisoned woman, lifelessly lying on a bed,
He had warned her about the book,
But now it was too late,
Vines were pushing their way out,
Of the book's spine,
Quietly,
On the bed,
Alone,
Eyes shut,
Mouth closed,
Undisturbed . . .

Georgia Przydatek (8)
Wantage CE Junior School

THE SOUNDS OF THE GREAT OUTDOORS

The birds twittering in a bliss,
voices talking in the mist.
A morning choir in the rise,
a rumbling beast in the skies.
The branches rustling in the wind,
the church bells ringing - royal din.
Sounds of joyous children chatting,
even though the traffic was flattering.
So does the boiler with the purring,
whizzing - wonders, sounds more luring.
The stampede of traffic coming day-by-day,
animals come in way-by-way.
Now this is what I call the great
outdoors!

Greg Barnes (11)
Wantage CE Junior School

PLAYGROUND SOUNDS

I walked into the playground,
And what could I hear,
The rumbling of cars, as they came near.

As I looked up, up in the air,
Concorde flew by, as fast as a hare,
Its engines roaring just like a bear.

High up in a tree,
Birds were making their nests,
While the sun was shining,
Towards the west.

As I looked towards the road,
A car was speeding by,
After this I heard a bird's cry.

In the morning,
When the playground is waking,
I find all the noises very stimulating.

Luke Wilkinson (10)
Wantage CE Junior School

FEAR

Fear is like the devil's friend.
Fear is like the devil's song.
Fear is like music dying.
Fear is like a rock falling.

Timothy Harris (9)
Wantage CE Junior School

PLAYGROUND SOUNDS

There I stood,
In the playground,
Not a sound to be heard,
Then suddenly whiz went a car,
Roar went another,
There I saw,
So many vehicles,
They were zooming,
Like a stampede,
Then the sound started to die down.

But it wasn't over yet,
A stamping sound was coming,
It went clump, clump, clump,
But then it stopped all so suddenly.

The birds were twittering,
Speaking loudly to their friends.

And all the time the trees,
The grass was swaying,
With a swishing sound calm.

A Concorde's engines grumbling,
It was definitely rumbling mournfully,
I thought it must have felt sad,
But then a joyful jet plane,
Cheering encouragingly,
Him to keep going.

The click of machinery,
Working hard,
The sound of old machines,
Left crying like a real person.

Christopher Moran (10)
Wantage CE Junior School

THAT GREEDY CAT

Where are those fish that swim about?
Wondered the cat that was short and stout.
He went into the kitchen and saw the tank.
Those lovely fish that swim about.

When he thought about fish, he licked his lips.
He imagined them lying in his dish.
He tried to think of a cunning plan,
To get them in the frying pan.

I must tell you about this cat.
His shape is rather round and fat.
Those lovely fish he didn't need,
He just wanted them for his greed.

He ran towards the tank and gave a jump
But he was much too big a lump.
He fell down and banged his head,
So his owner sent him straight to bed.

Claire Ord (9)
Wantage CE Junior School

SOUNDS

Behind the wall,
Birds sweetly sing like a church choir,
Gears change quietly,
As two cars crunch towards me,
Slowly creeping like giant snails,
Planes cross by like thunder,
Clashing, rumbling, rolling like drums,
From the classroom voices echo,
Children chattering, sound rises.

Lee Heggie (10)
Wantage CE Junior School

OUR BEAUTIFUL WORLD

Tiger saw man,
Tiger saw gun,
Tiger saw death coming -
Tiger was gone.

Extinction is forever.
Man is so clever
        with his gun.

Dolphin was gentle,
Dolphin was kind,
Didn't see the harpoon -
Diver didn't mind.

Extinction is forever.
Man is so clever
        with his harpoon.

Rainforest heard digger,
Rainforest saw axe -
Called out for mercy
As man broke their backs.

Extinction is forever.
Man is so clever
        with his axe.

So if you see an axe,
A harpoon or a gun,
Please don't pick it up -
Enough damage has been done.

Extinction is forever.
Man is *not* so clever
      with his tools.

The world is beautiful
And *we* are the fools.

Lucy Sanders (10)
Wantage CE Junior School

PLAYGROUND SOUNDS

As I was in the playground,
I heard the birds,
Chattering and whistling to each other.
Along with the birds,
I heard the cars roaring,
Down the road,
And the swishing of the aerial.

Concorde comes overhead flying like,
A train,
The pounding of its engine like,
Someone stuck in a box.

Footsteps clanking and clanging,
Along the path,
They thump like a heart,
Beating and pumping fast.
Footsteps skimming the concrete path,
A man walks away and everything
Is peaceful again.

Andrew Pickering (11)
Wantage CE Junior School

PLAYGROUND SOUNDS

I stood in the playground,
And guess what I heard?
Birds twittering and chattering,
Little ants on the ground scuttling.
I hear slight pads on the ground,
As tiny spiders hurry to catch their prey.
I hear the low hum of a distant robin calling to his friends.

Outside the gates the cars zoom by,
Deeply grumbling.
While up above Concorde consistently hums,
And roars like a lion waking from its sleep.
Across the road I hear a slight swishing,
As somebody's washing machine comes back to life.

We children were making noise too.
Christopher's deep coughing,
The slight squeak as the shoes scuff the ground,
The deep breathing of those who had a cold,
And the harsh scratching of pencil on paper.

The leaves were sitting in little clusters,
Swinging to and fro in the breeze,
Making a slight rustling sound.
Occasionally there was a gentle creak,
As the old tree bends in the wind.

The last thing I heard before I went in was:
A slight rustle, as the wind blew a white wispy web
of a spider to and fro.

Joanna Burch (10)
Wantage CE Junior School

PLAYGROUND NOISES

I stood in the playground and heard,
The birds gossiping and gabbling to each other.
I stood in the playground and heard,
Lots of lorries, cars and vans zooming past.
I stood in the playground and heard,
Nothing just a slight breeze,
After it was quiet and still.
I stood in the playground and heard,
An aeroplane droning across the sky,
Then . . . silence.

Lauren Walsh (10)
Wantage CE Junior School

PLAYGROUND SOUNDS

'It's playtime.'

The children's voices fill the air,
There's running and scurrying everywhere,
There are children kicking a ball,
And children chatting next to a wall.

'It's in time.'

The birds are chirping in the trees,
A dog barking in the distance,
And the crows are chit-chatting overhead.

Liam Amies (11)
Wantage CE Junior School

PLAYGROUND SOUNDS

Some people think the playground is a silent place,
When children go into work,
Sounds vanish without a trace.
But this is not what happens,
When children go into the school,
For if you think the playground is silent,
Then you are a fool.
The birds utter trilling warbles
Speaking in their own way,
It sounds charming and relaxing,
You could listen to it all day.
Planes,
Roaring like thunder gods,
Spilling out their rage,
Branches bending over and creaking with age.
Footsteps scuffing the tarmac path,
Footsteps scraping the tarmac path,
Cars, mumbling, grumbling, rumbling out their troubles to each other.
The aerial of a car whips the wind,
Like a slave-driver lashing out at slaves.
After that,
Nothing,
Silence,
Special silence,
Sacred silence.

Rebecca A Quinn (11)
Wantage CE Junior School

PLAYGROUND NOISES

Noises, on a sunny day,
Birds are chirping and chattering,
Sitting in the trees,
But not a sound of wind.

Vans and lorries zooming along,
Cars were rushing by.
Crows are cawing and calling,
Dogs barking and crying.

Children talking and screaming,
Balls are kicked and bounced around,
Footsteps up and down the playground,
With lots of noise.

Bianca Gartzen (10)
Wantage CE Junior School

SOUNDS IN THE PLAYGROUND

The playground's not a quiet place,
The sound drowns the teacher's voice,
Children bolting for the bounding ball,
Hitting it against the playground wall,
The postman flies past in his little red van,
Delivering to those expecting and those not.

    Crows calling coldly,
    Birds busily peaceful,

Boiler busily - at work heating the cold classrooms,
And vehicles skimming along,
But when it's time things calm down,
Just a man left in his garden peaceful and calm.

Robin Bolton (11)
Wantage CE Junior School

PLAYGROUND SOUNDS

I went into the playground
And what did I hear?
The chatter of birds, soft to the ear.
The cry and coo of the blackbird,
Twittering away,
As though he was thinking 'What a good day.'

I went into the playground
And what did I hear?
The rumble of traffic so very, very near.
The brakes screeching around the corner,
Like a scream from a haunted house
But others as soft and quiet as a mouse.

I went into the playground
And what could I hear?
Concorde flying so low, that we shrank in fear.
The planes soaring so high above,
I count them, there's ten
They disappear into the clouds and make it their den.

I went into the playground
And what did I hear?
People walking past me saying 'Not nice weather this year.'
The sound of children breathing,
So heavily
And all of them playing very merrily.

I went into the playground
And nothing was heard.
Not a plane, no traffic, not even a bird.
But then bit by bit,
It came back to life
And soon once again the noises were rife.

Sophie Webster (10)
Wantage CE Junior School

PLAYGROUND SOUNDS

I stood in the playground, I heard,
Birds cheeping and chirping,
In the high branches,
Of the old crinkly willow tree,
Like a piccolo, all different notes,
A, B, C, D, E,
As if the birds are reading,
A score of music.

Cars roaring and rumbling,
In a clamour,
On the wet, slippery roads,
Cars rushing about,
As if a race is on,
Water splashing, spraying up,
On their sides,
Like a garden hose.

Footsteps quietly tapping,
People walking to and fro,
Gravel grinding on the ground,
As people walk, tap, tap.

Branches and leaves,
Swishing and swaying,
In the rushing wind,
Blowing the yellow daffodils,
The wind, whistling,
Dashing through the tree branches,
Then back again to the tranquil silence.

Annie Berrett (11)
Wantage CE Junior School

SOUNDS

In between the playground and the courtyard,
I heard the birds singing in a choir
And then a car disturbed the birds' beautiful sound.
The car rumbled along the gravel.
Then a door opened with a screech,
Some people were walking on the gravel,
Then I heard a thud when a door closed.

In the kitchen, I heard someone lift up a box
And the cutlery jingling on the trolley,
Then I heard the car screeching away,
The birds started singing again,
In tune with a hammer hitting a large piece of wood.
Then two planes flew over like thunder dying away.

I heard the cars rushing to and from the motorway,
Drowning out the birds' song.
Finally I heard echoes coming from a classroom.

David Ralston (10)
Wantage CE Junior School

SOUNDS OF MARCH

Just through the gate,
We heard birds singing,
In tune like a choir.
Then gravel splattered
And gears changed with a gentle squeak,
Brakes smashed to a halt,
Doors clicked open and shut,
Men's voices, heels tapping, scraping
Like a drum beat.

Scot Mercer-Rolls (10)
Wantage CE Junior School

SOUND IS EVERYWHERE

The cold twang of the icy breeze,
Whispers soft lullabies to the world outside.
The trees slender fingers bend down to listen,
While the sharp fresh air invades the children's nostrils.

Suddenly, an increasing roar shatters the peace,
A metallic crashing, banging, speeds down the road without a care,
The sullen purring slowly dies away,
Then . . . silence.

A slow tuneful melody begins.
The other birds join in, a noisy buzz of cheerful chatter,
Twittering, screeching voices of song,
Hum in the slowly awakening air.

Steady footsteps sound on the tarmac,
Like the rhythmic knocking of a fist on wood.
A crunch, a swish, a growing beat,
A growing beat as the footsteps fade away.

Children stampeding back inside,
Quietly talking and laughing.
Taking a last listen and look,
Before they close out the outside sounds.

Sound is everywhere.

Catherine Rowe (11)
Wantage CE Junior School

SOUND

Screech!
A quirky bird starts chirping noisily,
Out flutters another bird,
Suddenly, out dashes a whole flock of birds,
Squeaking like mice.

Along rumbles a car,
Hissing like a snake,
Soon, the whole road sounds like a great stampede.

The church bells clang to a rhythmic beat,
Frantic footsteps of people walking past,
But then,
Silence.
No walking, talking or anything,
Just silence.

The wind ruffles the trees,
But no noise,
Unexpectedly,
There is the sound of a faraway car,
Getting nearer and nearer until . . .
Scrape!
It's back to normal.

Camilla Drury (11)
Wantage CE Junior School

OUTSIDE SOUNDS

Twittering, whispering, the birds are a glorious choir,
A plane rumbles by, a giant beast of the sky.
Chiming church bells, chattering children,
Voices in the distance, almost a whisper.

Branches rustling in the wind, as the trees speak in
their own silent whispers.
Stampeding traffic, clattering by,
I hear another giant beast zoom through the sky.

Aimee Talbot (10)
Wantage CE Junior School

THE PLAYGROUND

Pitter-patter footsteps,
Pitter-patter footsteps,
The cool breeze brushes past you like a feather,
Pitter-patter footsteps,
Pitter-patter footsteps,
The cool, whistling breeze, is all around you like an echo.

Crunchy, crispy footsteps,
Crunchy, crispy footsteps,
Crash! Splash!
Crash! Splash!
A huge iron beast is bumping noisily along the road,
Making huge fountains of water as it splashes in puddles,
Crunchy, crispy footsteps,
Crunchy, crispy footsteps.

Chirping, cheeping chaffinches,
Chirping, cheeping chaffinches,
Chattering children,
Clonking cars,
Rustling leaves,
People's footsteps,
Chirping, cheeping, chaffinches,
Chirping, cheeping, chaffinches.

Neil Ord (11)
Wantage CE Junior School

PLAYGROUND SOUNDS

Standing in the playground
Listening.
Listening to the sounds.
Birds, filling the air with
tranquil songs.
Hearing the cars
rushing like a bullet
from a gun, the door
slamming against the
wall, like the lights
going out in a room.
The boiler barely holding
the temperature that is like the sun.
The breeze, as
soft as a feather
touching your hand.
The shattered movement
of stomping children
break the silence, as they
discuss their work.

Christopher Knight (10)
Wantage CE Junior School

SOUND POEM

Fast, frenzied footsteps running, running.
Soft, sweet singing chirping, chirping.
Racers racing, stampeding sound,
Trees whispering all around.

Now there's nothing near, near.
Silent sound slippering here, here.
No racers racing or stampeding sound.
No trees whispering all around.

Alice Roper (11)
Wantage CE Junior School

STANDING IN THE PLAYGROUND

Noises, noises
Noises in the playground.
Birds chattering
Chattering loudly to their friends
Cars crashing, dashing by.
Lorries zooming, booming past
Trees dead still watching the world go by.

Noises, noises
Noises in the classroom
Children playing around,
Laughing and joking with their friends
Chairs scraping on the floor
The teacher standing in anger
Watching the children running past her.

> Noise.
> Noise.
> Noise.

Alice Hart (11)
Wantage CE Junior School

SOUNDS

The fresh smell of raindrops,
Hanging like a monkey
On a sharp blade of grass
As you breathe, a sharp breeze races in your mouth.

As you move, your feet crunch
On the gravel
We move to the courtyard
Listening to the boiler, purring like a cat.

The soft sweet birds, singing
Singing as if they are in a choir
Trees giving comfort to little
Baby birds, tweeting for their mother.

A loud sound of metallic
Crashing along the road
Disturbs all the birds
As the monster fades away.

Kayleigh Walton (11)
Wantage CE Junior School

THE SAD BEAUTY OF A CAT

My cat Smoky I miss him. He was so cute.
He ran to you when you called for him.
He had a beautiful face who always goes on a race
outside in the garden.
My dear cat that laid in the flowers, but I think he was a flower.
I love my cat who died by a car, you could run him so far.
I miss my dear Smoky, when he was mine he shot up like the sky.

My dear Smoky, bye-bye.

Lucy Jezzard (9)
Wantage CE Junior School

As We Walked Outside

As we walked outside we heard birds twittering in glorious choirs,
A humbling, rumbling beast circling the skies.
Cars whooshed by, faster than an eagle swooping the skies,
Leaves were swaying calmly in the trees.

As we walked outside we heard clattering lorries whizzing by,
The boiler purring softly, while the church bells chimed nearby,
Chattering children stampeding down the ramp,
Voices as quiet as a whisper float towards us,
As we walked outside.

Rachel Bowers (10)
Wantage CE Junior School

Weather Changes

Thunder and lightning roaring through the sky
Frightening the sun so it goes to hide
Like a lion scratching at the door
Breaking down branches of the trees
Worst still is the hurricane
Everybody running, screaming
Trying to get away
The soft humble snow
With children playing snowball fights and snowmen too
Now at last the sun is out
Everybody picnicking in the woods
Playing games all around
But wait
Here comes the eclipse
Now the world is dark and quiet.

Natalie Organ (9)
Wheatley Primary School

SPACE SHUTTLE

There's a space shuttle ready to launch,
In a California space port
Astronauts have boarded the shuttle
Fire crews are standing by
Everything is ready for when the space shuttle
Will launch into the sky.

10, 9, 8, 7, 6,
The tension is mounting
5, 4, 3, 2, 1 and 0
The space shuttle launches into the air
Goodbye space shuttle
Well may you fare.

Up it goes higher still
Up in clouds of smoke
Higher, higher
Out of sight
Leaving the Earth's atmosphere.
Will it ever return
To this space port here?

Jerome Thomas (10)
Wheatley Primary School   .

WAR

The war is over
Glory and happiness everywhere
Everyone out having parties
But not the ones still on the battlefield
Everyone is happy now
But not when they remember
The horrors of the terrible war.

Stephen Breisner (10)
Wheatley Primary School

WACKY WORLD

Wacky World is weird
It's somewhere in the sky
The town hall is tasty
Because it's a big apple pie.

Wacky World is weird
The people who live there
Are just basic pencils
With great big mops of hair.

Wacky World is weird
You simply must visit there
If you go you'll get a hotel
That's inside a giant pear.

Jonathan Rudgewick-Brown (9)
Wheatley Primary School

DUCK-BILLED PLATYPUS

A duck-billed platypus am I.
And what I'd like to know is why,
When all the animals were created,
My size and shape were not debated.
A cowboy job is indicated!
They made me of left over bits,
I think it really is the pits.

Caitlin MacGeorge (10)
Wheatley Primary School

DOLLY, MY HAMSTER

Dolly is my hamster,
He is extraordinarily light,
The colours of his fur are,
Brown and black and white.

Dolly is my hamster,
His nose if soft and pink,
His eyes are black and shiny,
But I've never seen him blink.

Dolly is my hamster,
He's never been known to bite,
He sleeps all day,
And is wild at night!

Eleanor Grebenik (9)
Wheatley Primary School

CATS

A lovely soft purr,
Twinkling eyes like stars,
Silky fur,
And twitching whiskers.

It cuddles up to you,
Like you're a warm blanket,
By a cosy open fire,
It could stay there all day,
If it could, all it would do
is purr, purr, purr.

Donna Jones (10)
Wheatley Primary School

OLD AND ALONE

I'm old and alone
With no one to talk to
I have got a house
But it's old and damp.

I'm old and alone
It's starting to snow
It's misty outside
And very cold.

I'm old and alone
I'm feeling quite poorly
I can't get out of bed
But no one cares.

I'm old and alone
It's Christmas Day tomorrow
I've bought a small tree
I've got no money left for presents.

I'm old and alone
It's Christmas Day today
I haven't received any gifts
Apart from a small card and a present.

I'm old and alone
There is snow and mist outside
But no one has called
Nobody cares about me.

Amy Hoidge Hughes (10)
Wheatley Primary School

THE SUPPLY TEACHER

The supply teacher comes in the room,
Everyone starts mucking about,
Trying to make the class go boom,
And then we made a roundabout.

Tying the supply teacher up,
Going to the playground,
Finding a cup,
And finding a pound.

We have lookouts at the door,
The teacher comes back,
We tidy up the floor,
We put the teacher in a sack.

Matthew Williams (10)
Wheatley Primary School

DRUMS

I was playing on some drums
Really liked them
They were good fun
From West Africa
Different to other drums
Better
Base, slap and tone
Most of my mates liked them
Some were big
Some were small.

Ollie East (10)
Wheatley Primary School

THE SPARROWHAWK

The sparrowhawk is
Like the wind
Swishing and swooping
Through the trees
Suddenly it sees
Its prey and
Dives down like
Lightning bringing sudden
Death to its
Victim.

Adrian Lanczak (10)
Wheatley Primary School

BUBBLES

Lots of bubbles floating in the air
Each one landing in a different place.
One on a shoe,
One on a mat,
One slowly floating down
Lands on a book,
It leaves a mark.
Another floating in the air
Pop, pop it disappears.

Sophie Court (9)
Wheatley Primary School

THE WIND IS A CHEETAH

The wind is like a cheetah
Jumping from roof to roof,
Howling through the streets.
It runs after its prey until it catches it,
It knocks down the chimneys with its
Paws and razor sharp claws,
It gradually dies down and it strolls into
Its cage and goes to sleep.

William Palmer (10)
Wheatley Primary School

THE STORM IS A BULL

The storm is a bull,
Charging again and again,
Banging on your door,
Keeping you awake,
Roaring away all night long,
Galloping down the street, bang, bang, bang,
Slowly he calms down, breathing heavily,
Then walks back to his field,
And lies down to sleep like a little lamb.

Rhian Littlewood (9)
Wheatley Primary School

THE JOURNEY

Under the ocean
Swimming through the sea
Come on a journey
A journey with me.

Up in the sky
Flying with the birds
Floating with the clouds
It's too incredible for words.

I'm as tall as a giant
I'm one centimetre small
I'm as tiny as an ant
I'm a hundred metres tall.

Up in the sky
Over creation
Over the seas
Of my imagination.

Claire Townsend (9)
Wheatley Primary School

THE SNAIL

I am a very slimy snail,
I leave a silver trail on the grass.
I don't make a sound when I
Slither on the ground.

Jade Hixon (9)
Wheatley Primary School

FELIX THE NUTTER

Felix has gone crazy,
He really is a nutter,
He'll get into the fridge,
And dribble on the butter.

When he wants his cat food,
He'll jump up at the wall,
Then he'll do crazy cartwheels,
And squall and squall and squall.

When he wants a rest,
He'll find a squodgy chair,
Then he'll go to sleep,
With his tummy in the air.

When he wakes up,
He'll want his sister to fight,
He will get her in a corner,
And bite and bite and bite!

When he's resting on a bed,
He'll scratch at your poor toe,
Then you have to push him off,
And then he's full of woe.

Felix is my darling cat,
He is my sweetie pie.
I love him very, very much,
Though you might wonder why.

Rebecca Murphy (10)
Wheatley Primary School

MY CAT SHANDY

My cat Shandy is black and brown
She's always happy, she never frowns
She's such a good cat
She waits by the door on a mat.

My cat Shandy is soft and cuddly
She comes up and jumps on me
She has a little wet nose
that sometimes glows.

My cat Shandy purrs silently
When she's hot she goes under a tree,
Then suddenly she goes to sleep
and I'm glad she's mine to keep.

Amy Thomas (10)
Wheatley Primary School

MILLENNIUM

The Millennium Dome is very bright with lots of colours like yellow
and white.
With lots of things to see and do, especially for me and you,
People will come from near and far, some by taxi, some by car.

Some may walk, some take the train,
But I don't think anyone will come by plane.

Louise Jones (8)
Wootton CE Primary School

THE MILLENNIUM DOME

I think the Millennium Dome is a great idea.
But it is a shame they don't have a Millennium Gnome to go with it,
if they did have a Millennium Gnome it would have to be exquisite.
With a lovely bright red hat,
and a nice white T-shirt, (not too tight)
big red boots,
and nice red trousers.
That's what I think is nice for the Millennium Gnome.
Just think next time it could be pink.

Emily Green (7)
Wootton CE Primary School

MILLENNIUM

Two thousand years have gone by,
During which time men have learnt to fly.
From flying small heights in a balloon,
To flying all the way to the Moon.
In the next millennium we'll go to the stars,
We'll visit Pluto, Jupiter, Saturn and Mars.
We'll holiday on a planet many light years away
And the sun will shine every night and every day.
When we look down from the sky we'll see the Millennium Dome,
This will always remind us of our beautiful home.

Chloe Atherton (8)
Wootton CE Primary School

THE NEW MILLENNIUM

It's the new millennium,
full of cheer.
Lots and lots of drinking beer!

Have a party,
lots of fun.
Celebrate the millennium!

Lots of celebrations,
in the street.
Where lots of friends go and meet,
going out for a millennium treat.
Go on, shoo! Go and eat.

Pop the cork!
Let it fly!
Hope there aren't any passers by.
Bang!
Explosions going on!
In the new *millennium!*

Alicia Clarke (8)
Wootton CE Primary School